Re-visioning Community Colleges

American Council on Education Series on Community Colleges
Series Editor: Richard Alfred

Titles in the Series

First in the World: Community Colleges and America's Future, by J. Noah Brown
Student Success: From Boardrooms to Classrooms, by Vanessa Smith Morest

Re-visioning Community Colleges

Positioning for Innovation

Debbie Sydow and Richard Alfred

Published in Partnership with

American Council on Education™

Leadership and Advocacy

ROWMAN & LITTLEFIELD PUBLISHERS, INC.
Lanham • Boulder • New York • Toronto • Plymouth, UK

Published by Rowman & Littlefield Publishers, Inc.
A wholly owned subsidiary of The Rowman & Littlefield Publishing Group, Inc.
4501 Forbes Boulevard, Suite 200, Lanham, Maryland 20706
www.rowman.com

10 Thornbury Road, Plymouth PL6 7PP, United Kingdom

British Library Cataloguing in Publication Information Available

Library of Congress Cataloging-in-Publication Data

Sydow, Debbie.
Re-visioning community colleges : positioning for innovation / Debbie Sydow and Richard Alfred.
p. cm.
Includes index.
ISBN 978-1-4422-1486-6 (cloth : alk. paper) -- ISBN 978-1-4422-1488-0 (electronic)
1. Community colleges--United States. 2. Community colleges--Evaluation. 3. Community colleges--
United States--Administration. I. Alfred, Richard L. II. Title.
LB2328.15.U6S94 2013
378.1'5430973--dc23

                                                                        2012045612

ACE   American
      Council on
      Education

Leadership and Advocacy

The paper used in this publication meets the minimum requirements of American National
Standard for Information Sciences Permanence of Paper for Printed Library Materials,
ANSI/NISO Z39.48-1992.

Printed in the United States of America

THE COMMUNITY COLLEGE SERIES

Community colleges currently enroll 6.5 million students in 1,200 institutions—one out of every two first-time students entering college and slightly less than one half of all undergraduate students in the nation. By 2016, they are projected to enroll 7.5 million students, many of whom will be minority, lower income, and underprepared for work and further education. They are the fastest-growing segment of higher education both in number of institutions and enrollment. Yet, remarkably, they are the least understood of postsecondary institutions in terms of literature and research describing their mission and role, organization and operations, and performance. This void invites quality scholarship on a segment of higher education in which interest is high and audiences are both substantial and growing. There is much in the higher education news about community colleges, but not the critical scholarship and analysis necessary to support and sustain dialogue about issues and challenges facing them.

The Community College Series is designed to produce and deliver books on current and emerging "hot topics" in community colleges, developed from a leader and managerial point of view. Our goal is to develop distinctive books on salient topics. Each book is expected to be practical and concise, provocative and engaging, and to address multiple dimensions of a topic. Most books are written by a single author—a college executive who brings expert and practical understanding to a topic; an academic or researcher who has a unique slant and bank of information to bring to a topic; a policy analyst or agency official who possesses critical insights into an issue; a think tank scholar who has the capacity to identify and examine a challenge or issue that is likely to confront community colleges in the future. To ensure practicality and different viewpoints, authors are expected to solicit and present ideas from a variety of perspectives and to include examples or case studies on how institutions and leaders might deal with the topic from a strategic and operational perspective. Finally, to ensure that each book brings maximum value to the reading audience, authors are expected to present original research and use out-of-the-box thinking in manuscript development. Each book is expected to represent the very best thought on a topic at the time of publication.

Richard Alfred, Editor, Community College Series

Contents

Foreword

Karen A. Stout

Today's community colleges seem ideally positioned to respond to our country's increasing demand for postsecondary skills development and higher education for more people at multiple points throughout their lives. Yet resources are limited and out of proportion with what are required for our sector to produce reasonable success rates, especially given the increasing diversity in academic preparation and support needs of our students. Successfully addressing this challenge requires innovation beyond incremental improvement. It requires re-visioning, making this book, *Re-visioning Community Colleges*, a must-read for those of us in the midst of leading this essential transformational work.

Because of our promise for success, community colleges are being recognized at many levels. Private funders are investing significantly in our work. Policymakers believe that expanded support for many of our promising innovations will create new scalable, sustaining, and systems-changing solutions to the affordable delivery of higher education and skills training. These funders and policymakers believe, as Clayton Christensen and others describe in a *Harvard Business Review* article titled "Disruptive Innovation for Social Change" do, that the community college model is a "catalytic innovation—one that is dramatically changing the shape of higher education in the United States by expanding access to and redefining the goals for advanced study."

Re-visioning Community Colleges makes a timely case that while we have been historically successful at adopting innovations such as online learning, dual enrollment, workforce preparation, and remedial education, we have not been successful at bringing these innovations fully to scale. We are, therefore, in the midst of an "unfinished revolution." It is time, according to authors Debbie Sydow and Richard Alfred, for a "no-holds-barred" analysis of the shape and future direction of community colleges, an analysis that despite our reluctance must focus on organizational redesign. As a sector, we must re-vision. As community colleges we must reimagine our futures. As community college leaders, we must lean into ambiguity, reject the status quo, and jump into action.

In many ways, *Re-visioning Community Colleges* is an excellent companion to the recently released report of the American Association of Community Colleges 21st-Century Commission on the Future of Community Colleges titled *Reclaiming the American Dream: Community Colleges and the Nation's Future*. The book's authors reinforce the clarion call of the 21st-Century Commission report for community college leaders to mobilize collectively to carry out the transformation agenda from the inside, one college at a time, but in unison as a sector. Just as the 21st-Century report is a call for colleges to redesign, reinvent, and reset, *Re-visioning Community Colleges* offers a compelling case to reexamine who we are, how we do business, and the results we deliver. Sydow and Alfred warn that the 21st-Century report is not a guidebook for future success, cautioning that "the Commission's recommendations must be seen as remedial, a catch up step for an enterprise producing outputs short of stakeholder expectations." I agree that we must go beyond the report to revitalize our colleges and that there is no exact prescription for moving forward because of the varying nature of our community colleges. I believe, though, that insights gained from reading *Re-visioning Community Colleges* combined with adopting the 21st-Century Commission report recommendations will offer practitioners possibilities for developing a pathway forward for building the capacity for change and innovation at their individual colleges.

In equally important ways, *Re-visioning Community Colleges* offers a new and valuable comprehensive account of the development of community colleges, cast in the context of today's challenges. Declaring that "community college leaders would be wise to take a lesson from history," the authors effectively frame the multiple paradoxes we face as leaders of community colleges. In a counterintuitive way, the authors challenge us to learn from the successes of the past even though these successes present a predisposition to incremental rather than disruptive innovation.

The authors urge today's leaders to look at our current state through the lens of competing paradoxes—growth and reduction, abundance and scarcity, continuity and change, access and success, tradition and innovation, competition and collaboration, convergence and divergence—and to understand that the choices we make as leaders in managing these contradictions will shape our colleges. There are at least two important takeaways in this discussion of paradox. First, the accretion model of curricular growth used at most of our campuses is not sustainable. We need strategic, demand-driven academic programming. Second, we have sophisticated models to respond to market needs to add new programs. However, we don't have robust models for doing program cost analyses, performance measurement, and other business practices that are required for us to be innovative, high-performing organizations. As a community college leader and practitioner, I found this chapter on managing paradox and building organizational capacity for change and innovation most engaging. It convinced me that despite our reluctance, we must begin to focus on full organizational redesign and not wait for incremental interventions to take hold on our campuses.

The authors build on this case for managing contradictions by dedicating a full chapter to highlighting ideas and practices of the most provocative thinkers and practitioners in today's community colleges. This chapter includes important practical examples of disruptive innovations in action. The examples can be studied and replicated at many of our colleges.

Finally, *Re-visioning Community Colleges* will also inform the recent rethinking of the design of community college leadership programs of all types. I agree with the authors' observation that our sector's "attachment to stability, to the status quo, is reinforced by leader's training and experience." To move forward with disruptive innovation, our leadership programs must focus more on managing and leading organizational redesign and on supporting leaders in managing through contradictions. *Re-visioning Community Colleges* is a must-read for those of us building our own internal leadership academies. It will be an assigned reading in our program at Montgomery because of its excellent accounting of the community college history and the case it makes that our unique characteristics, historically described as vulnerabilities, constitute fertile ground for future and necessary innovation.

I applaud Debbie Sydow and Richard Alfred for taking on this work at such an important time in the development of our colleges. They paint an important and new multidimensional picture of the community college organizational life cycle from our period of growth to a period of deepening maturity and stability to the present period of required renewal. *Re-visioning Community Colleges* makes a compelling and must-read case that addressing our challenges and renewing our organizations for relevancy will require innovation and disruptive innovation, well beyond the incremental improvements that many of us are now adopting. The book starts by asking the question: "Are community colleges an industry on the threshold of restructuring?" I finished the book convinced and motivated to be a force for change and restructuring rather than face a certain decline that our students and our country cannot afford.

Karen A. Stout, President,
Montgomery County Community College (Pennsylvania)

Acknowledgments

As lead author, acknowledgment and appreciation is first extended to Richard Alfred. In the summer of 2009 when I accepted a call to serve on the National Advisory Panel for the Community College Series, the decision was motivated by a long-standing interest in expanding the body of research-based literature available to community college leaders. As a veteran administrator, I know from experience that ongoing engagement with literature that critically analyzes extant issues in the higher education industry staves off ennui and improves job performance. In his capacity as chair of the National Advisory Panel, Dick urged me, challenged me, and ultimately convinced me to be among the authors contributing to the Series. Then he convinced me to serve as coauthor. The opportunity to coauthor a book with Dick Alfred was one not to be missed—a bold checkmark on my career bucket list. In an email note to my coauthor at an early stage of conceptualizing *Re-visioning Community Colleges*, I confessed to feeling like a sprinter who unwittingly finds herself lagging behind in a cross-country race, wondering if she has the stamina to cross the finish line. The iterative process of research, conceptualization, synthesis, writing, and revision of a full-length book requires different "muscles" and skills than those that I routinely exercise as a college president. Refocusing my own lens through the research and writing that went into this book has been both a humbling and an exhilarating experience, an experience that I would heartily recommend to my colleagues.

For enthusiastically supporting and encouraging my work on this book, I am forever indebted to the Onondaga Community College Board of Trustees: Chair Margaret "Meg" O'Connell, Donald Mawhinney Jr., Dr. Gary Livent, Connie Whitton, Steve Aiello, Allen Naples, Melanie Littlejohn, Dr. Donna DeSiato, and Student Trustee Patrick Caulken. Risk tolerance is indicative of a healthy and innovative organization, and trustees had no qualms about putting the institution "out there" as a case study. Onondaga faculty, staff, and students give life and character to the institution and to the vignette presented in the book. I am thankful to all of them for allowing me the privilege of serving in the role of president for twelve years, for it was from that vantage point that I formed many of the opinions and insights advanced in *Re-visioning*. The research underlying strategic planning efforts at Onondaga dovetailed perfectly with the questions and concepts explored in *Re-visioning*. Accordingly, appreciation is extended to Nicole Schlater, assistant to the president, and Agatha Awuah, vice president of institutional planning, assessment, and research. Nicole was a pitch-perfect sounding board and a rigorous editor throughout every phase of the writing process. Nancy Martone and Julie Hart in the president's office at Onondaga managed to maintain a perpetually pleasant and productive work environment. All of these individual and collective contributions added considerable value to the final manuscript.

As coauthors, we acknowledge the time, talent, and candor of each thought leader, scholar, foundation executive, and college president who contributed to what is, at its essence, a robust dialectic about innovation and the future of community colleges. Using data to improve institutional performance is at the heart of the work of Brian Bosworth, founder and president of FutureWorks; Stan Jones, president of Complete College America; and Josh Wyner, executive director of the College Excellence Program, Aspen Institute, and their work enriches any discourse on community colleges, including this one. Jamie Merisotis, president and CEO of the Lumina Foundation, and Anthony Bryk, president of the Carnegie Foundation for the Advancement of Teaching, are strategically advancing outcomes-driven change in sundry ways, not the least of which is investing the resources needed to support innovation. Presidents Karen Stout, Daniel Phelan, Carl Haynes, Mary Fifield, Jack Becherer, Martha Smith, Audre Levy, Eduardo Padron, Wright Lassiter, Sanford Shugart, Allatia Harris, Glenn DuBois, Ann McGee, Ann Kress, Donald Snyder, Linda Thor, Bert Glandon, Jim Catanzaro, Nancy Zimpher, and Scott Evenbeck are not only practicing CEOs of community colleges or systems, but also they are clear and compelling thinkers, which makes their willingness to contribute to a book about the future of community colleges all the more valuable. In the absence of their insights and thoughtful predictions, the ideas in this book would undoubtedly ring hollow.

Appreciation is extended to the Australian government for granting permission for on-site research by Debbie Sydow at selected Tertiary and Further Education (TAFE) institutions and in universities throughout New South Wales and Queensland. Special thanks is extended to Janine Schubert and Angela Jackson at the TAFE Open Learning Center in South Brisbane; Professor Janet Verbyla, deputy vice-chancellor for Global Learning and dean of Sciences at the University of Southern Queensland; Nigel Hill, director,

Wide Bay Institute of TAFE, Maryborough Campus; Professor Steve Bowman, chancellor of Central Queensland University; Gary Kinnon, director, Central Queensland Institute of TAFE, Rockhampton Campus; and Mark Harris, owner and director of Global Education and HR Consultancy Services, who served as an advisor and liaison on both continents. Everyone with whom we met and communicated, both face-to-face and electronically, was extraordinarily generous with their time and information, and the international perspective added considerable value to our work.

Individually, we acknowledge and thank those who contributed immeasurable personal and professional support:

Debbie Sydow: Harry Sydow, Mandy Allen, Audrey Allen, and William Allen—my solstice, equinox, and seasons complete.

Dick Alfred: My partner in life and work, Pat Carter, who is a constant source of inspiration and ideas. Debbie Sydow, whose intellect, analytical skills, and insight have made this book an invigorating experience from start to finish. And the many colleagues who have shaped my work—presidents, higher education academics, and graduate students—to whom I am eternally grateful.

Debbie Sydow
Richard Alfred
July 2012

On the Threshold of Restructuring

The core educational mission of colleges and universities is more important than ever—to the future of individuals, employers, and society. Increasingly complex problems in all sectors require that individuals continue to build new knowledge and skills throughout their lives. Despite the presence of over seven thousand higher education providers in the United States, the nation has lost its position as leader in the percentage of its population that has attained a degree, and the gap between the number of graduates and the projected need remains a concern. At the same time that wages and job opportunities for individuals without a college degree continue to decline, the costs of enrolling in college have pushed student loan debt to an all-time high of over one trillion dollars.[1] The current trajectory is not sustainable.

The emergence of land grant colleges after the Morrill Act of 1862 and the emergence of community colleges at the turn of the twentieth century represented an "innovation" in the higher education industry designed to address one of its first major challenges—expanding access to higher education in response to growing public demand and to industry needs for increasingly skilled workers. As community colleges and, indeed, the higher education industry as a whole struggle to navigate the high-stakes economic and political landscape of the twenty-first century, we have set out to explore current and emerging trends in the ways that community colleges—diverse and frequently enigmatic institutions—are, or could, adapt, innovate, and recreate themselves to meet the educational challenges of our day. Enormously successful in terms of their impact on expanding access to higher education, community colleges possess attributes that are uniquely aligned with the changing needs of students, communities, and employers. Yet they are besieged by challenges that may compromise the principles upon which they were established. Chief among them is a disjuncture between demand,

1

resources, and accountability that has brought community colleges to the threshold of restructuring. This disjuncture is not a passing phenomenon. It will defy quick fixes or easy resolution. For this reason, the time is right for a "no-holds-barred" analysis of the shape and direction of community colleges in a landscape of dramatic and unstoppable change.

Re-visioning seeks to portray what future success will look like for community colleges. Its objective is to present an unblemished view of current circumstances and conditions—both environmentally and institutionally—and then to adjust the lens to bring into focus what will likely occur in the distance of a decade or two. Predicting the future in a turbulent landscape is a tricky, even daunting, endeavor. For this reason, we have relied on colleagues to sharpen our view of the blurry outer reaches of the future. The ideas and insights of some of today's leading thinkers and practitioners appear throughout the book.

WHY NOW?

With domestic and global economies in disarray, the labor market in transition, and resources becoming increasingly austere, this is precisely the time to use lessons from our industry's past and the wisdom of contemporary leaders and scholars to chart a future course. This is, to be sure, a critical juncture for community colleges. On the downside, widespread funding cuts precipitated by the 2008 financial collapse and subsequent recession have exacerbated problems brought about by historic underfunding. And the recent enrollment boom—driven in part by the financial crisis and shifting demographics—is slowing. On the upside, community colleges have evolved into prominent players in the nation's effort to address and resolve issues of economic instability and global competitiveness. New resources are being invested, particularly in workforce training and initiatives designed to support improved college completion rates, by foundations (the Gates Foundation, Kellogg Foundation, Lumina Foundation, and Ford Foundation) as well as by corporations (Microsoft), government agencies (Department of Labor, Department of Education, and the National Science Foundation), and non-governmental entities. Multiple drivers are carrying community colleges in a fast-moving current of change, but the course and the destination have yet to be clearly determined.

Now is the time to re-vision, not only because the challenges facing our colleges are significant but also because the opportunities ahead are infinite. The changing economic and political climate presents new prospects as colleges seek to align programs and services with emerging needs. Consider the potential of:

- new programming in response to shifting industry demands and the emergence of new industries, such as alternative energies;
- new knowledge about what has worked and what has not relative to learning and completion;
- new students emerging from dramatic demographic shifts;
- new technologies that will profoundly impact and indelibly transform teaching and learning.[2]

This transformation can be left to powerful environmental forces already reshaping America's institutions, or it can be executed inside our colleges and carried out as part of a mission that fundamentally distinguishes community colleges from other higher-education providers. There really is no choice—we must carry out this transformation agenda from inside. And we can start by re-visioning who we are, how we do business, and the results we will deliver.

PAST, PRESENT, AND FUTURE

Past as Prologue

The rapid growth of higher education and of community colleges over the last three decades has created unprecedented opportunity for access. Opportunity has not been matched, however, by a corresponding increase in the number of learners earning postsecondary credentials,[3] and the average time it takes to complete a degree is increasing. Among students starting at four-year institutions, only 34 percent finish a bachelor's degree in four years and barely two-thirds (64 percent) finish within six years.[4] The statistics for community colleges are even worse. For newly entering students planning to obtain a degree, only 34 percent complete any degree within eight years of entering college.[5] In fact, many leave without qualifications: no degrees and often no credits.

As community colleges strive to meet the growing demand for postsecondary education and to improve completion rates, a glance back at their early vision can be instructive in developing a better understanding of how past and present conditions serve as a prologue to the future. The literature offers limited empirical evidence of the factors that helped and hindered the early development of community colleges. The challenges facing our colleges have been well documented, but only a handful of studies contribute to our understanding of the evolution, successes, and failures of community colleges. Very little research of consequence is in print, despite the fact that community colleges now enroll approximately 44 percent of all undergraduate students in the United States.[6]

In *The Diverted Dream: Community Colleges and the Promise of Educational Opportunity in America, 1900–1985* (1989), Steven Brint and Jerome Karabel tracked the evolution of community colleges from 1900 into the 1980s, and they argued that community colleges embodied an egalitarian promise, but at the same time reflected the constraints of the capitalist economic system.[7] In 2011, J. M. Beach built upon the work of Brint and Karabel in documenting "the institutionalization of the community college" as "a muddle of mixed motives and competing actors" represented by state legislatures, school boards, and university leaders who had a hand in the formation of junior college missions and funding structures.[8] Beach argued that despite the idealism reflected in epithets like "democracy's colleges," community colleges were established from the outset as underfunded, marginalized institutions in the well-established hierarchical system of higher education. Beach highlights the work of Cohen and Brawer (1982), Brint and Karabel (1985), Grubb and Lazerson (2004), and other scholars who have attempted to dispel the simple but popular notion that community colleges were created to democratize American higher education by providing equal opportunity for social and economic mobility.[9] These works helped to unmask the political, economic, and social forces that shaped community colleges over the last century, but they provided little by way of insight into the operating dynamics of community colleges. Rather, as is our thrust in the next chapter, their contribution has been to document the complex history of community colleges and the role that historical factors played in their development.

If the past is, in fact, a prologue to the future, then current political, economic, and social conditions portend greater numbers of students of diverse origin entering community colleges. Not only will they be diverse in race and ethnicity but also in academic preparation and service needs. The resources needed to serve these learners will be limited and completely out of proportion to the resources needed to produce reasonable success rates. It doesn't take much to figure out what this means for institutions and leaders. A "business as usual strategy" will not be sufficient to produce meaningful performance gains for institutions working in a landscape in which politicians and resource providers have dramatically changed the interpretation of success.

Paradox of the Present

Depending on how one defines success, the record of community colleges in today's landscape is mixed. The fact that roughly half of all college students now attend community colleges would seem to suggest that our colleges have become prime-time players. This is the first part of a paradox in which community colleges are embroiled. The dramatic enrollment growth that our colleges have experienced belies the very real influence of economic and political drivers. The lingering recession has prompted more high school graduates to enroll in college as a means of preparing for entry or, in some cases, deferring entry into the job market. The sluggish economy has forced more displaced workers to return to school to learn new skills and has enticed growing numbers of university students to "drop down" from four-year to two-year programs as a way of reducing expenses and the long-term burden of college debt.[10] This confluence of circumstances, while bringing visibility to the role community colleges play in enabling access to higher education for the populace, may also have created an enrollment base that is temporary and incapable of being sustained.

However, compared to students' overall number in community colleges, far too few of them who enroll actually graduate. Despite the personal and professional benefits, as well as the modest economic return that completing a series of college courses may offer, the large number of students who fail to complete college courses in an era when college graduation rates fall short of market demand for graduates is viewed not as a gain, but as lost opportunity costs—to individuals, employers, and communities. Community colleges face unique challenges in supporting completion that many four-year institutions do not. Yet, it is highly unlikely that four-year institutions could accommodate the millions of students who enroll at community colleges, and even if they could, there is little evidence to suggest they would achieve different results unless adequately resourced. The challenges facing public four-year institutions—which like community colleges face declining public investment and the consequences of mission sprawl—make it highly unlikely that four-year colleges will have the capacity to absorb additional learners even if they want to. To purport that access could be readily provided by traditional, four-year public colleges is not realistic today, nor has it ever been a valid assumption.

The second part of the paradox rests on the relationship among demand, value, and resources. When measured in relation to the resources needed to support enrollment growth, community colleges have not fared well. Postsecondary education is fast becoming a universal expectation, but as a policy matter, community colleges operate primarily on enrollment-based budgets that average about one-fifth of those of their four-year public counterparts.[11] In 2009 to 2010, the latest year for which Education Department data are available, colleges and universities spent $461 billion, with public four-year institutions spending approximately $235 billion and public two-year colleges spending just over $52 billion; a ratio that has remained relatively stable over time.[12]

Is the fate of community colleges then predetermined by a history of open access and its inherent challenges—volatile and anemic enrollment-driven funding, sprawling curricula and support services, and identity confusion? Or do their unique attributes and their focus on responsiveness to evolving community needs help to better position community colleges among various providers of higher education to adapt to the volatile conditions and rapidly changing needs of students and the nation? Do institutions delivering community-based curricula in flexible delivery modes to a highly diverse population have a unique ability to support learning in the information age? Community colleges would seem to be ideally positioned to respond to increasing demand for higher education for more people at multiple points throughout their lives. Enrollment patterns, however, will be affected by the rising cost of higher education against a backdrop of declining family incomes. And while recession-driven demand for lower-cost educational options has induced higher-income U.S. families to turn to community colleges as a viable option based on their value proposition, will expanded experience with, and exposure to, community colleges result in new loyalties that will reshape the enrollment decisions of a new generation of students?

Generational studies research would suggest a community college advantage. The brand consciousness of Baby Boomers and their tendency to equate value with price has given way to the more conservative path of saving and spending prudently by Generation Xers who today make up a significant portion of community college students and their parents. Even though the new generation of community college students, the Millennials, have spent substantial amounts of noncash money (online purchases, debit cards, and so on) at an earlier age than previous generations and may not be mindful of cost, their views about diversity and the value they place on heterogeneity would seem to add value to community college as an educational option for this generation of learners.[13] The next learner generation, labeled as Homelanders or Generation Z by some, is expected to be the most racially and culturally diverse generation in U.S. history simply because of migration trends within and outside of the nation's boundaries. For this reason, and in tandem with advances in global communication, this generation may be the most transient generation of learners ever. Community colleges, with their history and experience in serving and responding to the educational needs of diverse populations through flexible delivery systems, are particularly well positioned to continue to adapt to changing generational and demographic trends.

Turning to disparities in public funding between two-year and four-year institutions, there are indications that this gap may be shifting. Careful not to overstate its meaning or to suggest the emergence of a trend, encouragement can be taken from the fact that for the first time in recent history, perhaps the first time ever, the 2011 to 2012 budgets passed by state legislatures from California to Pennsylvania to New York contained cuts that were larger for four-year colleges and universities than for community colleges.[14] Likewise, as the nation seeks to reconcile the highest unemployment rates in a generation with workforce shortages in multiple industries, community colleges are receiving new infusions of funding to support innovative programs and continuous improvement measures through federal and state grants, as well as private funding by foundations, including The Bill & Melinda Gates Foundation and Lumina Foundation.

The third and final part of the paradox is realized in the juxtaposition of access and success. Having received accolades for years as an open-access portal to postsecondary education, community colleges today are focusing on success as much as access. There is a new and decidedly rigorous spotlight on community colleges today for organizational change efforts tied to completion agendas. Collaborative research programs initiated by organizations like the Carnegie Foundation for the Advancement of Teaching are beginning to build a small cadre of evidenced-based methods that community colleges are deploying in an effort to achieve breakthrough performance. Possessing the basic components needed to rapidly elevate educational levels of American citizens and to improve the nation's global competitiveness, community colleges are squarely at the center of national attention on the education front. They are being hailed by employers, the federal government, and foundations alike as the best hope for practical, innovative solutions to economic and political exigencies. At the same time they are faced with a mandate for improved performance and the expectation that completion rates will grow or consequences not altogether attractive will follow.

Portal to the Future

Looking to the future, in a 2011 report released by the Center for American Progress and Innosight Institute, Christensen, Horn, Caldera, and Soares argue that the higher education industry's most significant challenge, at its core, "is that of managing innovation effectively."[15] Asserting that frame-breaking change is the key to making a quality postsecondary education affordable, Christensen et al., define disruptive innovation as innovation that "replaces the original, complicated, expensive product with something that is so much more affordable and simple that a new population of customers in an outer circle now has enough money and skills to buy and readily use the product."[16] Explaining that new products typically start in an inner circle because they are "expensive, complicated to produce, and available only to the customers with the money to afford them and skill and access to use them," disruptive innovation occurs "when the products previously only available to a smaller, inner circle of individuals become affordable and accessible to those in the outermost circles."[17]

Based upon this definition, it is fair to say that the emergence of community colleges could be viewed as one of the "disruptive" innovations in the higher education landscape of the twentieth century. Community colleges introduced a modified higher education model by unbundling research from teaching and learning, by focusing on the first two-years of postsecondary education, and by presenting a different value proposition predicated on accessibility (open access), affordability, and practicality (applied degrees), rather than one centered on exclusivity and prestige. In the twenty-first century, community colleges have continued to adopt new innovations in an effort to improve access, and increasingly, outcomes. Many were early providers of workforce development programming and early adopters of online education, and in recent decades they have moved to capture the lion's share of the total undergraduate market in higher education, most of the workforce education market, and, more recently, online markets, all of which have contributed to explosive enrollment growth.

It would seem that despite an arguably inglorious past, community colleges have embedded in their DNA the ability to continue to evolve as provocateurs of innovation in higher education. There is ample evidence to suggest that this evolution is well underway and that it will continue into the foreseeable future.

The major premise of *Re-visioning* is that unique attributes that define community colleges, once viewed as outside of the mainstream and therefore "second-choice" institutions, are increasingly aligned with the needs of learners, making them, potentially, better positioned now more than at any other time in their history to achieve their unique educational mission. This depends, however, on the ability of our colleges to leverage their unique attributes to manage the contradictions embedded in their mission, resources, and systems.

Innovation and future success will be guided by daring and increasingly entrepreneurial institutions—those whose leaders and institutions are vigilant and disciplined in finding new revenue streams to fund community-based programming, aggressive in containing costs while insisting upon leveraged outcomes in student learning, and creative in developing new approaches to educational opportunity and academic quality.

However, even the most clear-eyed accounts of the ways in which community colleges have faltered and the ways in which they have acclimated to prevailing conditions are hollow in the absence of examples of new manifestations of the "vision" of community colleges in plans and innovations underway at institutions across the country. *Re-visioning Community Colleges* highlights ideas and practices of some of the most provocative thinkers and practitioners of the day. Current conditions and new approaches are analyzed through the lenses of scholars, futurists, and resource providers. It is our hope that this publication will help to crystallize a new vision for community colleges by highlighting ideas and practices that will be integral to their role as innovators in American postsecondary education.

NOTES

1. Vickie Elmer, "Dealing with Student Debt," *New York Times*, April 26, 2012, http://www.nytimes.com/2012/04/29/realestate/mortgages-dealing-with-student-debt.html (accessed August 29, 2012).

2. Diana G. Oblinger, "IT as a Game Changer," in *Game Changers: Education and Information Technologies*, ed. Diana G. Oblinger (Lawrence: Allen Press/EDUCAUSE, 2012), 37–51.

3. U.S. Department of Education, National Center for Education Statistics (NCES), Integrated Postsecondary Education Data System (IPEDS), Spring 2011, Graduation Rates and Institutional Characteristics.

4. Richard Arum and Josipa Roksa, *Academically Adrift: Limited Learning on College Campuses* (Chicago: University of Chicago Press, 2011), 54.

5. James E. Rosenbaum, Julie Redline, and Jennifer L. Stephan, "Community College: The Unfinished Revolution," *Issues in Science and Technology*, http://www.issues.org/23.4/rosenbaum.html (accessed June 7, 2012).

6. American Association of Community Colleges, "2012 Community College Fact Sheet," 2, http://www.aacc.nche.edu/aboutcc/pages/fastfacts.aspx, based on AACC analysis of NCES (2009), IPEDS Fall Enrollment Survey.

7. Steven Brint and Jerome Karabel, *The Diverted Dream: Community Colleges and the Promise of Educational Opportunity in America, 1900–1985* (New York: Oxford University Press, 1989), 5–11.

8. J. M. Beach, *Gateway to Opportunity?: A History of the Community College in the United States* (Sterling, VA: Stylus Publishing, 2010), xxxi.

9. Beach, *Gateway to Opportunity*, 41–68.

10. Tom Kucharvy, "The Community College Contribution," The Future of U.S. Knowledge Work in a Global Economy (blog), Beyond IT, August 8, 2010, http://beyond-it-inc.com/GKEblog/growing-importance-of-community-colleges.html (accessed August 29, 2012).

11. Mary Beth Marklein, "U.S. Community Colleges at a 'Turning Point,'" *College Blog*, *USA Today*, August 1, 2008, http://www.usatoday.com/news/education/2008-07-22-comcolmain_N.htm (accessed August 29, 2012).

12. U.S. Department of Education, National Center for Education Statistics, Integrated Postsecondary Education Data System (IPEDS), Spring 2005 and Spring 2010, Enrollment component; and Spring 2006 and Spring 2011, Finance component.

13. The Center for Generational Studies, "Views on Money," *FAQ* (2011), http://www.generationaldiversity.com/index.php?/faq.html (accessed August 29, 2012).

14. David Moltz, "'Triage' Funding for Community Colleges," *Inside Higher Ed*, March 31, 2011, http://www.insidehighered.com/news/2011/03/31/state_budgets_and_community_college_funding (accessed August 29, 2012).

15. Clayton M. Christensen, Michael B. Horn, Louis Caldera, and Louis Soares, "Disrupting College: How Disruptive Innovation Can Deliver Quality and Affordability to Postsecondary Education" (Washington, DC: Center of American Progress and Innosight, February 8, 2011), 2, http://www.americanprogress.org/issues/2011/02/disrupting_college.html.

16. Christensen, Horn, Caldera, and Soares, "Disrupting College," 13–14.

17. Christensen, Horn, Caldera, and Soares, "Disrupting College," 13.

Chapter One

Breaking Barriers, Boundaries, and Beliefs

Most four-year institutions in the United States were founded on the organizational, curricular, and operational structure of the "colonial colleges" of the seventeenth and eighteenth centuries. Conversely, community colleges grew out of burgeoning demand for access to postsecondary education and changes in the economic, political, and social fabric of the United States in the twentieth century. This chapter provides an overview of the evolution and the emergence of the core characteristics that have come to define community colleges. Its intent is to provide context for the main premise of this book, that the unique characteristics historically described as vulnerabilities for community colleges constitute fertile ground for innovation in the future.

EMERGENCE OF COMMUNITY COLLEGES

The establishment and evolution of community colleges has been well chronicled, as have its political and philosophical underpinnings, as told by Walter Crosby Eells in *The Junior College* (1931), Edmund Gleazer in *This Is the Community College* (1968), Arthur Cohen and Florence Brawer in *The American Community College* (1982), Thomas Diener in *Growth of an American Invention: A Documentary History of the Junior and Community College Movement* (1986), Steven Brint and Jerome Karabel in *The Diverted Dream: Community Colleges and the Promise of Educational Opportunity in America, 1900–1985* (1989), George A. Baker III in *A Handbook on the Community College in America: Its History, Mission, and Management* (1994), and more recently by J. M. Beach in *Gateway to Opportunity? A History of the Community College in the United States* (2011).[1] These authors and others described the development of community colleges as one part of an increasingly structured and highly integrated system of education largely built in twentieth-century America. This system did not evolve by chance. It was influenced by distinct national movements, including the expansion of the public education system, increased professional standards for teachers, the vocational education movement, and an ever-expanding demand for adult and community education.[2] The value of five decades of work by multiple authors extends vastly beyond historical accounts of the development of community colleges. It is realized in the capacity of different authors to identify and document problems and contradictions inherent in the community college role that stem from a history of perpetual tension between lofty ideals and marginal resources.

No matter how the story is told or who tells it, all seem to agree that community colleges, since their inception, have been shaped—and in some instances misshaped—by ideological, economic, social, and political forces. Over the past century, these forces have functioned as enabling conditions for the community college movement, yielding success in numbers but leaving institutions habitually vulnerable to external forces beyond their control.

A UNIQUELY AMERICAN SYSTEM OF EDUCATION

It was at the turn of the twentieth century, amid growing demand for access to higher education and a growing concern among four-year institutions about resources and capacity, that community colleges were born. The backdrop was a national push to expand the number of citizens with secondary and postsecondary education to advance the growing industrial economy. Community colleges were not an isolated educational phenomenon. As described by Ratcliff (1984, 1986, 1987), junior colleges came into being as an extension of K–12 school systems and compulsory secondary education.[3] Growing numbers of high school students set educational reformers in search of a more efficient system to absorb graduates who were in the market for postsecondary credentials. The shifting economy—from agrarian to industrial—and compulsory secondary education, which was legislated in the early twentieth century as a way to advance the economy, brought the need for a new educational system to the forefront of public attention. In a climate of national optimism and economic progress, education for everyone was a notion whose time had come. Compartmentalizing or "boxing" the functions and roles of each discreet level of education contributed to an "efficiency" that aptly reflected a core value of the industrial age.

Contextually, community colleges did not emerge from a conceptual model that was painstakingly designed and constructed by educational experts, nor did the institution emerge as a domestic replica of organizations already in existence in Europe and other parts of the world. Rather, the basic concept and organizing principles of the community college emerged in response to immediate social and political demands, discreet problems, or, as some have argued, from crises. For example, Ratcliff highlights the fiscal challenges of many traditional four-year institutions as a major factor in the birth of the community college:

> The Panic of 1894 . . . led to some of the first formal thinking about two-year colleges. Reverend J. M. Carroll, president of Baylor University, had convened a convention of Baptist colleges in Texas and Louisiana that year. The convention recognized that there were insufficient finances and students to support the numerous, small Baptist colleges in the two states. Carroll advanced a pragmatic suggestion. The smaller Baptist colleges would reduce their curriculum to the first two years of college, and Baylor would accept their students . . . Thus, the two-year college was born.[4]

Community colleges functioned from the outset as institutions tailor-made to address extant social, economic, and political issues. Consequently, they emerged in varied forms, depending on the conditions of the time and place in which each institution was established. Many were built from universities, others out of secondary schools, some from normal schools, and a few from private organizations and nonacademic technical institutes. "The administration of two-year or junior colleges and their organization within school districts or state systems of education also varied from region to region" on the basis of local conditions and needs.[5] Joliet Junior College, for example, was established in 1901 in Illinois by the Joliet Township School Board to offer postsecondary courses beyond high school to a growing population of high school graduates. The oldest continuously operating two-year college in the nation, Joliet is widely recognized as one of the first public junior colleges with the primary mission of offering the first two years of a four-year degree.[6]

Economic, social, and political circumstances—both national and regional—would continue to act as primary determinants of community college organizational models, leading to multiple variations on a common theme through successive eras and into the present day. Even today, no two institutions are identical, and most still largely reflect the history and circumstances of the period in which they were chartered and the locale in which they operate. It is this rich variation between and among two-year colleges across the country that has enabled them to survive and thrive over the past century.

CURRICULAR SPACE AND CRAWL

The chronicling of curricular development and enrollment growth throughout three generations of community college history—from 1901 to post–World War II, 1950 to 1980, and 1980 to the present day—begins with a fundamental duality that is embedded in the community college curriculum. Examine almost any community college's menu of offerings, and the standard fare is likely university transfer curricula—freshman- and sophomore-level courses—alongside programs designed for career preparation. Although some junior colleges (transfer curricula) and technical colleges (vocational curricula) remain, most community colleges today are considered to be comprehensive. Still, university transfer programs and technical/vocational programs tend not to exist in balance. Most catalogs will present a smattering of remedial, workforce, and community-based courses and programs, reflecting the "erratic mixture of curricula" that has existed from the beginning,[7] but the real bread-and-butter, credit-bearing curricula remain divided into two primary categories: general studies for university transfer and applied sciences or technical/vocational for career preparation. The technical/vocational track was slow to emerge, however. Similar to the emergence of community colleges as an organizational construct, the curriculum emerged in response to economic, social, and political circumstances of the time.

STAGES OF DEVELOPMENT

First Generation: Identity Crisis (1901 to Post–World War II)

When Joliet Junior College opened its doors in 1901, demonstrating that a well-equipped public high school could offer college-level courses equal to those offered by a university, it became a prototype for junior colleges.[8] Its primary mission was to offer the first two years of a baccalaureate degree. The fact that prestigious universities such as the University of Chicago and Northwestern University accepted Joliet's courses as equivalent to their own firmly established the "transfer" function of two-year colleges. Even though many of the first two-year colleges were technical institutes—for example, Lewis Institute in Chicago, founded in 1896, and the Bradley Polytechnic Institute in Peoria, Illinois, founded in 1897—the dominant curricular offering until the mid-twentieth century remained general education or university transfer.[9]

From the outset, universities were quick to voice support for the establishment of two-year colleges, which advanced their goal of increased selectivity. In describing the dominant perspective of university leaders of the early 1900s when junior colleges were first taking shape, Beach highlights the words of Ray Lyman Wilbur, president of Stanford University, who, in 1927, described two-year colleges as follows: "While serving as a trying-out place for the youth of the country, the junior college, by relieving the university of the elementary work of the first two years, can set the American university free to carry out its own great purposes."[10]

Lest there be confusion about the student populations to be served, college and university leaders were careful to delineate discrete functions for each sector. For example, James Madison Wood, president of Stephens College, speaking at the 1940 annual meeting of the American Association of Junior Colleges (AAJC), implored two-year colleges to focus their attention and efforts on "the great numbers of students who drop out of conventional high schools and colleges" and "play a major role in attacking this problem . . . They need not allow themselves to become enmeshed in the interests and objectives of the traditional college."[11]

In an attempt to clarify its purpose and plant a stake in the ground with regard to university equivalency curricula, American Association of Junior Colleges had in 1922 defined the junior college as "an institution offering two years of instruction of strictly collegiate grade." During that same decade, Walter Crosby Eells, Leonard I. Koos, and Doak S. Campbell moved to articulate a unique role for community colleges in providing terminal degrees designed to prepare students for direct entry into "semi-professions."[12] Yet student surveys taken at the time revealed that the vast majority of students (58 percent to 80 percent) had enrolled with the intention of continuing their studies at a four-year college, and far fewer students (only about 1 percent of respondents surveyed in California in 1924) identified occupational training as an advantage of the community college.[13]

Nevertheless, in response to shifting economic conditions (for example, high rates of unemployment), AACC in 1925 expanded the mission of two-year colleges to include "the larger and ever-changing civic, social, religious, and vocational needs of the entire community." Walter Crosby Eells's 1931 book, *The Junior College*, asserted that "the transfer function was important, but because of the fact that the majority of all junior college students will not and should not go on to a university, junior colleges needed to organize more fully trade and semi-professional terminal programs that would meet local and regional labor market needs."[14] In retrospect, Eells's logic would appear to be sound given 1930 census figures indicating that less than 10 percent of the population of the country would be needed for jobs in the professions.[15]

Thus began the vocational movement. Brint and Karabel point to AAJC's *Junior College Journal*, founded in 1930 under Eells's editorship, as "a crucial forum for promoting vocational curricula," noting that "among the seven 'representative junior colleges' featured in early issues of the 1932 *Journal* were at least four that could be considered highly vocationalized for the period."[16] By the mid-1930s, policymakers largely took it for granted that terminal vocational programs were central to the curricular portfolio of two-year colleges, not merely a less popular alternative to university parallel programs.

The influence of college and university leaders and AAJC in the early decades of the community college movement is well documented. Other forces were at work, however, that contributed to the shape and functioning of developing institutions. Among them was the influence of funding on curricular development. Early funding models in fast-developing community college states (California, Michigan, Missouri, Illinois, Texas, and Iowa) were enrollment driven. Regardless of curriculum, colleges received public funds on the basis of tuition and/or a formula that simply counted heads or full-time-equivalent students (FTES).[17]

Therefore, although developing "semiprofessionals" through career and technical curricula gave community colleges a new target population and an expanded mission, it was enrollment that drove curricular development and expansion. Regardless of the fact that two-year college leaders of the time "embraced the logic of vocationalism, by the 1930s, they had come to believe that the decided lack of student enthusiasm for anything other than college-transfer programs was the principal problem facing two-year institutions."[18] Despite repeated efforts on the part of community college leaders, administrators, and counselors in the 1920s and early 1930s to "dampen the enthusiasm of junior college students for academic courses that paralleled those of four-year colleges," students continued to enroll in transfer curricula.[19] In the absence of changes in funding formulas that might have enticed institutions to rethink their programming and enticed students and their families to choose technical/vocational curricula, university transfer curricula continued to dominate.

Simply stated, the push toward a more diversified curriculum—specifically the push to redirect university transfer enrollment and to expand technical/vocational enrollment—was not an easy sell, despite pressure from Eells and other higher-education leaders. Although community colleges were prepared to supply the programming, it was demand that lagged. Surveys of students at California junior colleges in the 1920s revealed that their primary reasons for attending junior colleges were to save money (60 percent) and to prepare for university transfer (58 percent).[20]

Nevertheless, influenced by widespread unemployment during the Great Depression, community colleges began to shift their focus to preparing people for jobs. What emerged was a national vocational movement. Developing "semiprofessionals" (a term widely used until after World War II) gave community colleges a new target population and an expanded mission. Their role in the vocational movement gained momentum with the release of a June 1932 report on public higher education in California declaring that the primary role of two-year colleges should be the provision of terminal degrees. A series of policy reports issued by AAJC in 1941 further solidified the vocational role of junior colleges.[21]

In 1937, AAJC established a policy committee, later renamed the Commission on Terminal Education, whose charge was to study "successful vocational education programs that might serve as models for member institutions."[22] Signaling an interest in two-year colleges as "potential developers of mid-level manpower," a $100,000 grant from the Rockefeller-funded General Education Board (GEB) funded the study and related activities designed to promote terminal education.[23] The grant supported the publication of three monographs published in 1941—including one titled *Why Junior College Terminal Education?*—which was based upon a survey conducted by Eells in 1940.

By the close of the decade, at least one terminal program was offered at 70 percent of the nation's two-year colleges. "Many of the techniques that helped transform the junior college into an institution oriented to vocational education—elaborate guidance procedures, surveys of employer demand, placement services, follow-up studies, citizen advisory boards, and the development of a 'community service' identity—were developed and perfected during the 1930s by administrators in a handful of California and Chicago area junior colleges."[24] Still, the problem of supply and demand remained.

Leaders of the time were not uniform in their focus on the technical/vocational movement and curriculum. Some envisioned a more comprehensive curriculum and role for the two-year college. For example, in 1936 a two-year-college president in Pennsylvania, Byron Hollinshead, wrote an article that emphasized the institution's role in "meeting community needs": "It should serve to promote a greater social and civic intelligence . . . provide opportunities for increased adult education . . . provide educational, recreational and vocational opportunities for young people . . . and be closely integrated with the work of the high school and the work of other community institutions."[25] This is one of the earliest uses of the term *community college*, and it marked Hollinshead as one of the "early visionaries who perceived a mission beyond 'two years of the four-year college.'"[26]

Regardless of curriculum offered—transfer, vocational, or both—community colleges proliferated during this period. The Great Depression, then, brought an unexpected two-part boost to the community college movement. Because of limited job prospects, young people had few alternatives to pursuing higher education. The largest boost came between 1933 and 1939 after state legislatures had time to respond to the twin pressures of increased demand and fiscal stress by authorizing the establishment of new or expanded two-year colleges. "In these six years, sixty-five public junior colleges were founded . . . by 1940 one student in ten was enrolled in a two-year institution (calculated from the U.S. Office of Education 1944, 4, 6)."[27]

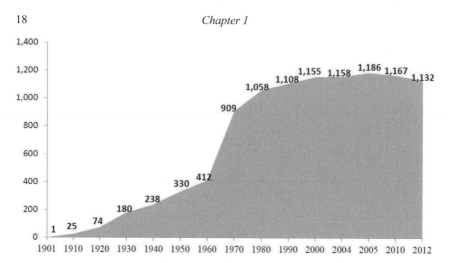

Figure 1.1.   Number of Community Colleges

Second Generation: Degree and Program Maturation (1950 to 1980)

In the first half of the twentieth century, vocational, technical, and preprofessional certificates, and two-year general education programs leading to an associate degree, were particularly relevant to a country in transition as a result of urbanization, industrialization, and economic development. Junior colleges established themselves as adaptive and pragmatic organizations, responsive to economic, political, and social conditions in their communities and the educational needs of a diverse population seeking postsecondary credentials. Throughout this fifty-year time period, over eight hundred public two-year institutions were established and two-year colleges were disaggregated from high schools as a separate educational entity. With this change in affiliation came the beginning of a new status and identity for two-year colleges, which up to this time had remained a largely ill-defined and misunderstood member of the higher education community.

In post–World War II America, the expanded mission and accompanying curriculum envisioned by Hollinshead and others were codified in a 1947 report titled *Higher Education for American Democracy*. The Truman Commission on Higher Education produced this report, and one of its hallmarks was a reference to two-year colleges as "community colleges." The Commission promoted the provision of education to a diverse population of learners at little or no cost, and attributed to community colleges five primary roles:

> First, the community college must make frequent surveys of its community so that it can adapt its program to the educational needs of its fulltime students . . . Second, since the program is expected to serve a cross-section of the youth population, it is essential that consideration be given not only to apprentice training but also to cooperative procedures which provide for the older

students alternative periods of attendance at college and remunerative work. Third, the community college must prepare its students to live a rich and satisfying life, part of which involves earning a living. To this end the total educational effort, general and vocational, of any student must be a well-integrated, single program, not two programs. Fourth, the community college must meet the needs also of its students who will go on to a more extended general education or to specialized and professional study at some other college or university. Fifth, the community college must be the center for the administration of a comprehensive adult education program.[28]

The ideas and ideals set forth in the Truman Commission report, particularly the provision of low-cost education to a diverse citizenry, reflected the optimism and prosperity that abounded in post–World War II America, a period of significant economic growth and expansion. Economist Richard Freeman and others referred to this period as the "golden age" for college graduates— an age in which salaries rose more rapidly for college graduates than for any other group. So it was in this fertile ground that the Commission redefined and replanted the seed of a "terminal" degree by describing "terminal education as a degree completion program that combined general 'social citizenship' education with vocational education for a semi-profession."[29] This attempt to promote a hybrid curriculum, one that would help to advance vocationalization by blending it with general education, failed to achieve its intended goal. The strong labor market for college graduates of the day actually "led to a decline in the proportion of vocational students enrolled in two-year colleges, from about one-third in the immediate pre-war years to less than one-fourth by the early 1960s."[30]

Unfettered by specificity regarding a curriculum of study, the GI Bill of 1944—one of the major higher-education acts in American history—made higher education affordable to returning veterans. Also at this time, the socioeconomic makeup of two-year college students changed. Pre–World War II students came largely from middle-class backgrounds. In the first ten years after the war, "students from lower middle- and working-class backgrounds made up the majority, perhaps as much as two-thirds, of the new students entering public two-year colleges."[31] These and other factors (for example, educational needs of the postwar baby-boom generation) contributed to explosive growth in community colleges during the highly unsettled period of the 1950s and 1960s. In large part due to affordable tuition and the proximity to home, by 1958, public two-year colleges enrolled almost one-third of entering college freshmen.[32] Rapid growth in the midst of social and political upheaval led to the program's proliferation, more diverse student populations, and mission creep—the modern-day community college, as we know it, had become an educational reality.

It is important to note that studies of the time continued to demonstrate that community college transfer students performed as well as, or better than, their four-year and university counterparts, adding legitimacy to what remained the dominant curriculum track well into the twentieth century.[33] Still, despite a short-lived Cold War–induced opposition to narrow skills training among some community college leaders in the late 1940s and 1950s, by the 1960s several states had converted their specialized vocational and technical schools into comprehensive community colleges. In North Carolina, for example, a 1962 Governor's Commission recommended that "the state develop one system of public two-year post–high school institutions offering college parallel, technical-vocational-terminal, and adult education instruction tailored to area needs."[34] This policy report and subsequent action revitalized the terminal degree with a blended vocational and general education curriculum as a viable model.

National commissions tended to look favorably on the community college during this period. "In 1960, the Rockefeller-sponsored Commission on National Goals predicted that two-year colleges would soon enroll more than 50 percent of the students entering college for the first time."[35] And a report by the Carnegie Commission on Higher Education, focused on policy recommendations for restructuring higher education in California, argued that community colleges should be linked to their communities and funded by local, state, and federal sources. The report urged both occupational and general education curricula.

A grant award of $750,000 from the Kellogg Foundation in 1965 (later raised to $1.5 million) was awarded to the American Association of Junior Colleges to support the development of semiprofessional and technical programs, which Brint and Karabel described as "a crucial event in AAJC's long-standing vocationalization campaign."[36] The Higher Education Act of 1965 made community colleges eligible to receive 22 percent of the authorized "developing institutions" funds, which they used, in part, to introduce new curricula and to develop cooperative arrangements with businesses and employers.

AAJC's decades-long advocacy efforts were clearly successful in convincing influential opinion leaders, funders, and policymakers that terminal programs at community colleges could address critical national problems as is evidenced by state, federal, and private funding directed in support of vocational programming during this period. By the early 1970s, corporations such as Ford, General Motors, IBM, AT&T, and Olin-Mathieson began to award grants in support of community college programs designed to prepare a trained workforce, signaling that semiprofessional or terminal programs were now at the core of the curriculum.

The still emerging U.S. system of higher education was heavily influenced during this period by a 1970 report from the Carnegie Commission on Higher Education (*The Open-Door Colleges: Policies for Community College*), which stated that "the ultimate objective" of all two-year college programs is "preparation for an occupation" and recommended "coordinated efforts at the federal, state, and local levels to stimulate the expansion of occupational education in community colleges."[37] Indeed, states took on a central role in funding community colleges in the 1970s, and as timing would have it, the economic turmoil of the period would influence both the level and focus of funding. As states competed to attract businesses and jobs, state-sponsored training programs were included in recruitment packages, and in states such as Ohio, North Carolina, South Carolina, and Tennessee, community and technical colleges were tapped to develop and deliver those programs.[38]

In response to the weak economy and growing economic insecurity among students, enrollment in occupational programs at community colleges grew from fewer than one-third of students to over 50 percent by the late 1970s.[39] At the same time, enrollment in transfer programs fell, and "the overall rate of transfer to four-year colleges and universities plummeted to an all-time low. Hoping to use higher education as a vehicle of upward mobility, many community college students ceased to believe that a bachelor's degree was the pathway to a better life."[40] A lingering recession and high unemployment rates left individuals and families questioning the return on investment or value of a baccalaureate degree, particularly liberal arts degrees not designed to lead directly to employment.

> Driven by difficult economic conditions, the Congress and other federal agencies of the time embraced the concept of the "educational marketplace." Legislation was enacted that effectively shifted federal dollars away from institutions and directed them, instead, to greater numbers of students through grants, work/study, and loans . . . It was this loss in federal support, combined with a drop in the number of college-age students, that spawned the lifelong learning or recurrent education movement of the 1970s and 1980s. . . . Adults were encouraged to use the community college (and other institutions of higher education) as educational cafeterias. "Take some courses, stop out, and come back for more" was the educational marketer's creed.[41]

These policies worked to the advantage of community colleges given their diverse portfolio of academic programs and services and their characteristic responsiveness. Even as the growth of four-year colleges slowed during the 1970s, two-year college enrollment continued to grow. Many enrolled to escape the Vietnam-era draft, or upon their return from military service. In addition, remedial courses and programs expanded in the 1970s, largely in response to growing numbers of nontraditional and socioeconomically disadvantaged students lacking preparation for college-level courses. In 1977 to 1978 nearly one in three mathematics classes taught arithmetic at a lower level than college algebra, and 37 percent of English courses were offered at levels below general college grade.[42] Interestingly, remedial courses offered at the college level were not a new development, but community colleges began to assume substantial responsibility for this market as early as the 1970s in response to shifting economic conditions and demographic trends.

By the end of the twentieth century, community colleges virtually owned the developmental education market, which grew into a $1 billion industry by 2008 when 40 percent of all college students took at least one remedial course.[43] Leaving aside the broader question of learning outcomes at the secondary level, this demonstrated a brand of entrepreneurialism that served community colleges well upon entering the post-9/11 recession of the twenty-first century. Community colleges were the sector of higher education to first tap into the adult learner market, perhaps influenced by those who "rejected the notion that American education was carried out in a three-layered hierarchy, running from primary school through graduate school."[44]

> This . . . represented the "core," but it overlooked a "periphery" in which over 60 million adults pursued learning opportunities very important to their lives. Moses challenged the monopoly that the educational establishment had over public policy and public resources. His views suggested that, although declining numbers were projected in graduates from high schools [in the 1980s] and that enrollments of conventional students in colleges and universities would decline, the need and demand for educational services would continue to mount.[45]

The second generation of community colleges (1950 to 1980) was largely defined by rapid expansion of academic programs and services in response to swelling enrollments. According to government statistics, a new two-year college campus opened at a rate of more than one a week from 1956 to 1960 (U.S. Bureau of Census 1975), and degree-credit enrollments at two-year colleges more than tripled between 1960 and 1970, from 451,000 to 1,630,000.[46] It was largely in the 1970s that the role of community colleges became firmly established within the U.S. system of higher education. Comprehensive community colleges with multiple educational missions serving a diverse array of students and community needs became an integral part of state systems of higher education. Beach sums it up as follows: "Community colleges began taking on the chaotic characteristics of a shopping mall."[47]

Third Generation: I-Dominant Information Age (1980 to the Present)

A whole new frontier for growth and expansion opened at the beginning of the 1980s for a sector that had become adept at stretching its boundaries to embrace new ideas, new opportunities, and new learners. Compelled by enrollment-based funding models to remain in a perpetual growth mode, the last two decades of the twentieth century would introduce a wide array of technologies, enabling community colleges to transcend barriers of time and space to accommodate growing demand. By the 1980s, economic, political, and social conditions would lead to new partnerships with high schools, four-year colleges, and businesses and industry, contributing to the expansion of mission and resulting in continued enrollment growth and increased student diversity.

The 1980s brought new opportunities and challenges to a sector of higher education that had struggled to establish a separate and distinct role from secondary schools and universities. During this decade partnerships with these entities presented a whole new avenue for expansion. Community colleges expanded upon their "dual" programming in both technical/vocational and transfer curricula, and they assumed responsibility for a more comprehensive curriculum in response to social, economic, and political demands. Rightful ownership of curricula, however, was called into question. A report produced by the Brookings Institute in 1981 suggested that in anticipation of a decade of declining enrollments and increased competition among higher education providers, "most students would be better off pursuing a baccalaureate degree in a 4-year college or university."[48] The report recommended that community colleges focus on vocational-technical, remedial, and non-credit community service programs. Irrespective of whether the report played a causal role, vocational enrollments in the early 1980s exceeded transfer enrollments at many community colleges, and some of the more popular career programs, such as nursing and other health programs, were in such high demand that students had to be turned away and redirected into transfer courses and curricula.

Some view the successful vocationalization of the community college curriculum as akin to relegating community colleges to the "second- and third-rate educational functions" that L. Steven Zwerling described as inferior space in the "educational caste system."[49] Others, such as researchers Belkis Suazo deCastro and Melinda Mechur Karp of the Community College Research Center for the Office of Vocational and Adult Education, point to the ways in which vocationalization, particularly as it evolved in response to industry demands, aided important collaborations with business and industry and secondary schools and universities. "Industry demands are pushing community colleges to create new degree programs that offer industry-recognized credentials and facilitate transfer between sub-baccalaureate and baccalaureate degree programs."[50] In a very real sense, the vocational movement propelled by the 1990 Carl D. Perkins Vocational and Applied Technology Act and federal funding to support career and technical programs, and Tech Prep, readied community colleges to respond to the Obama administration's call to produce increased numbers of "credentialed" workers. Stated differently, demand finally caught up with the structure that evolved to support it in America's community colleges. This sector produced credentials that prepared people for real jobs—768,803 certificates[51] in 2008 to 2009 and over 464,000 associate degrees[52] in career and technical fields in 2009 to 2010. Some states were quick to connect the dots between industry-based community college programming and economic development, and they used the former to advance the latter.

For example, in Massachusetts, the community college mission and the curricular manifestation of that mission was defined and driven in accord with industry needs. By 1980 Massachusetts governor Edward King, "an early convert to the idea of a high technology–dominated future in Massachusetts," had convinced the state legislature to establish a single board, the Massachusetts Board of Regents of Higher Education, and to appoint several executives from the advanced technology industry to the Board. The influence that this Board would exert on college programming and enrollment in Massachusetts was extraordinary, and the result was nothing short of transformational.

> The Regents established guidelines for campus budget preparations . . . Decisions on new requests . . . were entirely at the Regents' discretion . . . For the first three years, the highest-priority items were always the same: new instructional programs in engineering, computer science, and allied health. Throughout the system, curriculum development fell into line with the new emphasis.[53]

In the final decades of the twentieth century, community colleges offered an endless array of industry-specific program options ranging from customized contract training to consortium models serving specific industries to traditional applied science courses and programs. By 2004, more than 75 percent of community colleges offered contract training courses (Government Accountability Office 2008), a trend that was even more pronounced in rural areas, where more than 90 percent offered such courses.[54] Researchers have documented the growth in two-year degree and certificate programs to prepare individuals for careers in information technology and for emerging "green" jobs in sustainable design and construction, environmental testing and remediation, renewable energy, and other related fields.[55]

The advent of the twenty-first century further accelerated opportunities for colleges to engage in collaboration to deliver industry-specific programming in support of workforce and economic development. Industry demands pushed the creation of new degree programs offering industry-recognized credentials and facilitating the transfer between secondary, associate, and baccalaureate degree programs. The post-9/11 economy and the financial crisis of 2008 resulted in level or reduced appropriations to most already underfunded community colleges—a circumstance that encouraged colleges and other educational institutions to find ways to pool their resources.[56] At the same time, community colleges experienced a surge in student enrollment, driven, in part, by a sluggish economy and high rates of unemployment. "The result was a 'blending' of institutions with the line between high school, community colleges, and four-year colleges becoming progressively indistinct."[57]

Community colleges have a long history of partnering with four-year colleges through articulation and transfer agreements, and more recently with university centers. They have also partnered with high schools through shared facilities and programming, and more recently through Middle College, dual enrollment and Tech Prep. Their history of partnerships with employers is rich in the form of internships, contract training, and other workforce initiatives. The downside of such partnerships is that they can and sometimes do result in curricular sprawl and confusion.

> It should be noted that partnering with other institutions has the potential to significantly impact the mission of the community college. It calls into question the fundamental nature of publicly-funded two-year institutions of higher education. What is the purpose of the community college? And does it change when colleges start to meld with other institutions?[58]

Crucial to curricular development and delivery in the first decade of the twenty-first century was the ever-expanding bandwidth that supported media-rich online resources and new communication applications like Facebook, Twitter, and LinkedIn. The devices for using these technologies became smaller and more affordable thanks to nanotechnology, thereby opening up alternative delivery systems for a wide range of academic programs. Community colleges were quick to tap these new opportunities. According to a 2007 report by the Sloan Consortium, nearly 20 percent of all U.S. higher education students were taking at least one online course in the fall of 2006.[59] Two-year institutions had the highest growth rates and accounted for more than half of all online enrollments between 2001 and 2006. By contrast, "baccalaureate institutions began the period with the fewest online enrollments and have had the lowest rate of growth."[60]

Traditional operations such as libraries, bookstores, and even classroom instruction have been called into question as transitions to digitized texts, e-readers, open courseware, and online or hybrid course/content delivery have occurred with astonishing alacrity. Habituated to respond quickly to new opportunities, community colleges have embraced new technologies, which are particularly accommodating of the core mission to deliver programs to anyone, anytime, and anywhere.

Even as community colleges grapple with how to structure and finance programs and support services to meet student needs and help them transition to four-year institutions and the workforce, enrollment has continued to grow. In 2000, community colleges enrolled nearly six million students and nearly 40 percent of all undergraduate students in the United States.[61] According to a report issued by the Pew Research Center, 10.9 percent of all eighteen- to twenty-four-year-olds (3.1 million) were enrolled in a two-year college in October 2007, and by October 2008, that number hit an all-time high of 11.8 percent of all eighteen- to twenty-four-year-olds, including disproportionately high numbers of ethnic minorities.[62] More than a decade of tuition increases exceeding rates of inflation at four-year institutions and the economic recession beginning in 2008 contributed to an influx of students enrolling in community colleges, even as anemic state budgets forced reductions in funding for these institutions.

ACCESS TO OPPORTUNITY: REALITY OR ILLUSION?

When they first arrived on the scene at the turn of twentieth-century America, community colleges challenged long-held beliefs about who could attend college, eliminating admissions barriers and expanding the boundaries of higher education to include anyone demonstrating the ability to benefit. From their beginning, community colleges have attempted to serve as a vehicle for opportunity and the Jeffersonian Ideal. The belief among citizens that education supports the public good has helped to fuel the overall growth and expansion of education. In addition to the Jeffersonian view that a democratic citizenry must be an educated one, the notion of equality of opportunity and mobility are deeply ingrained in the American psyche and value system. After the Industrial Revolution, as the economy became increasingly mechanized and society increasingly urbanized, the notions of equal opportunity and social mobility intertwined with access to education. It is not surprising, then, that the very structure of the educational system that was established in the late nineteenth and early twentieth centuries, and that remains largely unchanged today, functions as a ladder designed to accommodate upward mobility.[63]

In the literature of the past one hundred years, much has been made of this egalitarian ideology, its manifestations in practice, and, more recently, of the failure of community colleges to achieve what is perceived to be an underlying promise that every individual who demonstrates the ability to benefit cannot only enter the door but actually leave with a credential in hand. Some have questioned the degree to which community colleges have served as the gateway to opportunity they were designed to be, and others have questioned whether they were designed to do anything other than reinforce the existing socioeconomic order.

In the 1970s and 1980s, researchers began to challenge the notion that community colleges served as gateways to opportunity, arguing that they instead served in effect, if not in purpose, to track individuals into low-paying jobs. Zwerling and Brint and Karabel were among the first researchers to suggest that community colleges created the illusion of upward mobility by channeling students away from higher-cost four-year colleges that served as a gateway to higher income and the professions, and channeling them into lower-cost institutions where students were less likely to earn a credential or complete a four-year degree. Zwerling typified this perspective on community colleges in his scathing 1976 analysis of the role and function of community colleges relative to social and economic mobility. In *Second Best: The Crisis of the Community College*, Zwerling asserted that the "class-based dropout rate at community colleges is a deliberate process of channeling students to positions in the social order that are deemed appropriate for them."[64]

Whether deliberate or not, there is ample evidence indicating that the open door of community colleges has turned into a revolving door for too many learners over the course of history (see figure 1.2). High attrition rates remain a primary concern today. A 2009 Brookings Institution report entitled *Transforming America's Community Colleges: A Federal Proposal to Expand Opportunity and Promote Economic Prosperity* suggests that "U.S. higher educational attainment, long considered a ladder to economic and social success, has stalled, and now reinforces inequalities between rich and poor America." The researchers conclude that although community colleges represent an "affordable, accessible route for a wide spectrum of students to further education and well-paying, high-demand jobs," low degree completion rates "raise serious challenges for public policy efforts to achieve robust, broad-based economic growth."[65]

Attrition rates tend to be even higher for students who are categorized as socioeconomically disadvantaged, a population that has traditionally favored the low-cost, open-admission, higher-education option provided by community colleges. Since the 1980s, community colleges have tended to enroll increasing numbers of socioeconomically disadvantaged students relative to other institutions of higher education.[66] Population demographics alone account for at least a portion of the high attrition rates at community colleges, as attested by research findings that reveal a direct correlation between socioeconomic status and educational attainment at all levels. The 2008 report of the Spellings Commission on the Future of Higher Education found that:

- low-income high school graduates in the top quartile on standardized tests attend college at the same rate as high-income high school graduates in the bottom quartile on the same tests;
- only 36 percent of college-qualified low-income students complete bachelor's degrees within eight-and-a-half years, compared with 81 percent of high-income students;

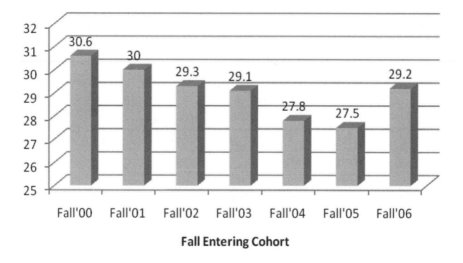

Fall Entering Cohort

Figure 1.2.   Three-Year Graduation Rates

- by age twenty-five to twenty-nine, about thirty-four of every one hundred whites obtain bachelor's degrees, compared with seventeen of every one hundred blacks and just eleven of every one hundred Latinos. [67]

The high rate of attrition among students across all sectors of higher education has become a topic of national discourse since the release of the Spellings Commission report, particularly in the face of increasing concern about the ability of the nation to remain globally competitive. Completion rates are only one measure of success, however, and a degree in the absence of knowledge and skills has limited value. The Commission urged colleges and universities to "continue to be the major route for new generations of Americans to achieve social mobility," but it warned that "the economic benefits of a college degree could diminish if students don't acquire the appropriate skills." [68]

Today public concerns about completion rates at community colleges has widened to include concerns about the extent to which colleges and universities are helping students to learn. In *Academically Adrift: Limited Learning on College Campuses*, Richard Arum and Josipa Roksa assert that the results of research they conducted using the Collegiate Learning Assessment serve as an indication that "large numbers of U.S. college students . . . are failing to develop the higher-order cognitive skills that college students should master." [69] In reviewing socioeconomic background data for the study participants, Arum and Roksa found that socioeconomically disadvantaged students achieved lower scores at the outset of the college experience, and at the conclusion of their studies they remained unequal, and in some instances even further apart, from students of higher socioeconomic status. This, of course, heightened concerns about the effects of college and what institutions were doing to mitigate disparities, let alone to serve as avenues of mobility.[70]

Setting aside the question of what is being learned and the inherent challenges of measuring learning, there is ample evidence to suggest that real economic gains do accrue to those who complete higher education credentials at all levels. It would seem, then, as is so often the case, the reality about the role of community colleges in either advancing or retarding social and economic mobility lies somewhere in the middle. Given the lack of hard data measuring the real value that community colleges have delivered as a rung on the American education system's K–16-plus ladder of equal opportunity and upward mobility, we are left with evidence that has contributed nothing more than contradictory opinions and beliefs.

A July 2009 headline in *Time* asked, "Can Community Colleges Save the U.S. Economy?" The article explored the growing enrollments at community colleges and their increasingly important role, as well as their unique challenges.

> The President hasn't forgotten about the 30 or so community colleges he visited during the 2008 campaign. These institutions are our nation's trade schools, training 59% of our new nurses as well as cranking out wind-farm technicians and video-game designers—jobs that, despite ballooning unemployment overall, abound for adequately skilled workers. Community-college graduates earn up to 30% more than high school grads, a boon that helps state and local governments reap a 16% return on every dollar they invest in community colleges. But our failure to improve graduation rates at these schools is a big part of the achievement gap between the U.S. and other countries. As unfilled jobs continue to head overseas, Obama points to the "national-security implication" of the widening gap. Closing it, according to an April report from McKinsey & Co., would have added as much as $2.3 trillion, or 16%, to our 2008 GDP.[71]

Fitzpatrick described "chronically cash-starved, two-year schools" that receive an average of just 30 percent of federal funding per student allocated to state universities even though they educate roughly the same number of undergraduates. Further, she noted that "two-year schools have been growing faster than four-year institutions, with the number of students they educate increasing more than sevenfold since 1963, compared with a near tripling at four-year schools." Still, federal funding for four-year schools has increased over the past twenty years, while funding for community colleges has held virtually steady. In fact, in 2009 federal funding accounted for only about 15 percent of total community college revenues (including financial aid).

The authors of the Brookings Report, *Transforming America's Community Colleges*, also highlighted the disparity between flat federal investment in community colleges and skyrocketing community college enrollment, which grew more than any other sector between 2000 to 2001 and 2005 to 2006, with an increase of 2.3 million students.[72] Noting that "community colleges receive less than one-third the level of direct federal government support as do public four-year colleges," the report highlighted community college vulnerability to fluctuations in state and local government spending, which on average comprise nearly 60 percent of their revenues.[73] The authors also pointed to evidence suggesting a correlation between funding and degree completion and recommended increased federal investment.

When it comes to tuition revenue, a 2011 survey by Sallie Mae revealed significant shifts in higher education spending among American families, including a decline in average spending. Despite the recession, between 2008 and 2010 families spent more on college, but they spent 9 percent less in the 2010 to 2011 academic year.[74] The report attributed the decline to a number of factors, including a movement among families in all income brackets away from four-year colleges to lower-cost community colleges. The percentage of high-income families enrolling in community colleges nearly doubled from 12 percent in 2009 to 2010 to 22 percent in 2010 to 2011.[75] According to the survey, families relied more heavily on grants and scholarships, which comprised 33 percent of all college spending—up from 23 percent in 2009 to 2010. Additionally, 46 percent of families received aid—up from 30 percent the previous year.[76] Despite relatively stagnant funding since the 1980s, community colleges have continued to expand programs and services over the past three decades.

ACCOUNTABILITY: MEASURING SUCCESS

In the face of expanding opportunities for growth and development, community college leaders would be wise to take a lesson from history. The preceding overview of curricular growth and expansion depicts a model of development that Robert Dickeson describes in *Prioritizing Academic Programs and Services* as an "accretion model."[77] Models of this type are not sustainable, particularly in periods of diminished public funding, for the simple reason that they are counterbalanced by mounting emphasis on accountability and increased demand for programs that prepare individuals with skills and credentials in newly emerging fields. As new courses and programs are added to the portfolio of college offerings over time and a modicum of courses and programs are eliminated, even on the basis of decreased demand, fixed costs exceed resources, and the business model is compromised. If course catalogs are generally reliable sources of information for comparing academic offerings at most community colleges, the picture is one of continuous decade-to-decade growth, not strategic, demand-driven academic programming. Institutions add programs because of a genuine desire to be of service, but growth, whatever its form, is an all-consuming drive for community colleges. Accretion models can lead to a loss of focus if not balanced by resources and accountability.

Renewed focus becomes a clarion call as education providers grapple with an obsession with testing and performance measurement that began in the 1980s. The controversial presidential commission report, *A Nation at Risk*, was released in 1983, launching America into "one of its periodic debates about the condition of the educational system. Initially this debate focused on elementary and secondary schools, but in recent years it has come to encompass the nation's colleges and universities as well."[78]

Accountability invariably takes on a new urgency and utility in times of economic downturn. It operates against a backdrop, however, of gains in learning outcomes that are difficult to document and achieve in institutions with ambiguous goals and unclear technology. In an *Achieving the Dream* policy brief released in 2005, state systems of performance accountability for community colleges were reviewed with a focus on the impacts—both intentional and unintentional—and lessons for policymakers. Among other findings, state performance accountability systems were found to be "inadequately funded, and unsteadily implemented."

> The emphasis on quality and getting a return on investment for public dollars led to the rise of performance accountability systems for higher education in the 1990s. The goal was to make higher education institutions demonstrate how well they were performing by citing not enrollment growth but rather gains in student learning, graduation rates, and placement in good jobs. The hope was that performance accountability—particularly if institutional funding were tied to it—would lead colleges and universities to become much more effective and efficient, doing better despite lagging or even declining state funding.[79]

Caution regarding "significant negative unintended outcomes" was advised. Even though the study found that community colleges have made changes in their structure and operations to achieve specific state goals, such as increased student retention and graduation rates, improved remediation, and better job placement, performance accountability systems appear to have limited impact on student outcomes.

As states grapple with systems for funding based on performance, the push for higher education accountability continues to gain momentum at the federal level. Pointing to the 2008 report by the Spellings Commission on the Future of Higher Education and its recommendations for improved cost management and value-added measurement of student learning, Dickeson described the mounting pressure being applied by the federal government to refocus higher education on cost efficiency and quality relative to learning outcomes.

> What the last half-century has wrought . . . are the increasing demands made by the federal government for information, compliance, and action . . . it should be clear to the higher education community that new expectations for quality assurance, accountability, and productivity are changing the sense of relative independence higher education has enjoyed . . . In its most fundamental form, the basic public policy question is reduced to: What are we getting for our money?[80]

Indeed, the Spelling Commission Report addressed the shortcomings of the nation's system of higher education and the consequences of those shortcomings both to individuals and the nation. Emphasizing the connection between education and economic competitiveness, the report sounded an alarm by stating that even though for more than a century the United States has educated more people to higher levels than any other nation, for the first time other countries "are now educating more of their citizens to more advanced levels than we are. Worse, they are surpassing us at a time when education is more important to our collective prosperity than ever."[81] The report criticized not only declining graduation rates relative to enrollment growth but also the performance of college graduates: "Unacceptable numbers of college graduates enter the workforce without the skills employers say they need in an economy where, as the truism holds correctly, knowledge matters more than ever."[82]

The Spellings Commission urged higher education to change from "a system primarily based on reputation to one based on performance and the creation of a robust culture of accountability and transparency throughout higher education."[83] The report's recommendations included increasing college completion rates, particularly among low-income Americans, by strengthening the relationship between secondary and postsecondary systems. It recommended that institutions reduce costs to make higher education more affordable through means such as increasing the high school–based provision of college courses and increasing need-based financial aid. It recommended that colleges ensure that graduates have the "critical thinking, writing and problem-solving skills needed in today's workplaces" and that "workers at all stages of life" have the opportunity to "continually upgrade their academic and practical skills" by "providing financial and logistical support for lifelong learning" and by providing "flexible credit-transfer systems that allow students to move easily between different kinds of institutions."[84] The report advocated for increased transparency and accountability, including measuring institutions on a "value-added" basis that takes into account a student's academic baseline when assessing results.[85]

The Commission urged the use of technology to "share educational resources among institutions" and to implement "distance learning to meet the educational needs of rural students and adult learners, to enhance workforce development," and to "improve student learning, reduce instructional costs, and meet critical workforce needs." It also urged colleges to use "learner-centered principles drawing upon the innovative work already done by organizations such as the National Center for Academic Transformation."[86]

In a sense, all institutions of higher education, particularly community colleges, have been understandably lulled into an illusion of success based on growth alone. The preceding century tells a story of the phenomenal rise of the higher education industry. For community colleges, growth has been stimulated by social, economic, and political circumstances that have served as enabling conditions for expanding not only their curriculum and programs but also their student populations. Indeed, community colleges have developed exceptionally sophisticated models and systems for adding new programs and delivery modes in response to demand. In general, however, they have not developed robust models and systems for conducting market studies, cost analyses, performance measurement, and other business practices that will prepare them to become the innovative, high-efficiency, high-performance institutions of the twenty-first century.

UNCONTROLLED SPILLWAYS: THE RISE TO INDUSTRY DOMINANCE

From the outset, community colleges have functioned, for lack of a better analogy, as uncontrolled spillways. An uncontrolled spillway does not have gates; rather, when the water rises above the lip of the spillway it begins to be released from the reservoir. Throughout their history, community colleges have functioned as institutions that stand ready to absorb swells of college-going students when other educational "reservoirs" are unable or unwilling to accommodate them. This along with advocacy, good timing relative to environmental forces and trends, and responsiveness in programming has driven a growth trajectory that is dramatic and episodic.

As discussed above, economic, social, and political shifts have also contributed to growth spurts at various points throughout succeeding eras and into the present day. Community colleges emerged in the early 1900s to serve a nation in need of more skilled workers for the industrial age. In the 1930s, Depression-era unemployment rates caused community college enrollments to swell, and high unemployment along with the GI Bill drove a post–World War II community college enrollment boom in the 1940s. In the 1960s and 1970s, baby boomers, returning Vietnam veterans, and those seeking to escape the Vietnam conflict pushed community college enrollments higher still. The late twentieth-century/early-twenty-first-century shift from an industrial to a knowledge economy and the seemingly insatiable need for new technology workers created another spike. And today, the post-9/11 recession and its accompanying high unemployment rates and major industry shifts, have driven community college enrollment to a record level.

Community colleges are now a dominant force in higher education. Today, more than 40 percent of undergraduate enrollment is comprised of community college students. The sheer size, scope, and market penetration of community colleges within the higher education industry are evidenced by the fact that nearly one in five Americans who earned doctorates in 2008 attended a community college at some point, and nearly 40 percent of Native Americans and more than 25 percent of multiracial Americans who earned doctorates attended community colleges at some point.[87]

The downside of the "big dog" syndrome—inefficiencies of accretion, inadequate quality assurance, vulnerabilities of inertia, and more—is clear, but there is also an upside. For example, size matters when it comes to influence, particularly political influence. Having finally established an identifiable brand, community colleges have generally enjoyed a favorable position at the federal, state, and local levels of government as they have become more clearly understood as low-cost workforce education providers. As the dominant industry sector, community colleges now have considerable influence on companies that supply products, equipment, and technologies for higher education. This is significant in that innovation will be driven by

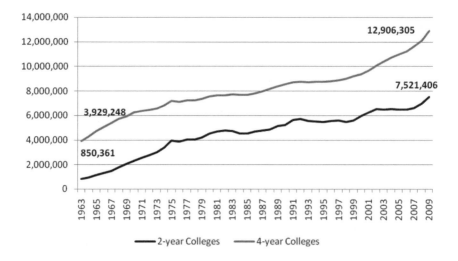

Figure 1.3.   Total Fall Enrollment in Degree-Granting Institutions by Type of Institution

technology (for example, open source courseware) in the future, and that technology will be influenced, in part, by its primary users. The sheer range and diversity of programs represented in community colleges is a strength, as diversification supports broad market penetration and protects against the vulnerabilities of specialization. Experience in serving large, diverse populations of students is another asset; national demographic trends are expected to undergo a major shift, and community colleges are well positioned to respond. Vast numbers of ubiquitous community college campuses—large and small—located in rural, suburban, and urban areas throughout the country, and the capital investment they represent, render these institutions a virtually indispensable asset. Scale is a strength, particularly as part of a distributive, local service model.

Despite these favorable conditions, the problem of student attrition remains a major concern for community colleges, particularly those striving to achieve high performance outcomes. The demand for accountability will likewise apply even more pressure on community colleges to provide evidence of student success. The problem is that many factors contributing to high rates of attrition remain beyond the control of community colleges. A 2009 report by Public Agenda, "With Their Whole Lives Ahead of Them: Myths and Realities about Why So Many Students Fail to Finish College," explored the characteristics of college students today and the barriers that stand in their way to degree completion. They include the following:

- Among students in four-year schools, 45 percent work more than twenty hours a week.
- Among those attending community colleges, six in ten work more than twenty hours a week, and more than a quarter work more than thirty-five hours a week.
- Just 25 percent of students attend the sort of residential college we often envision.
- Some 23 percent of college students have dependent children.[88]

The Spellings Commission report acknowledged the difficulty of evaluating the impact of community colleges, stating that institutional assessment is complicated by the diversity of the students served, the unique characteristics of the regions in which they are embedded, and the diverse goals and needs of their students and communities. Still, as part of the enterprise of American higher education, community colleges can benefit from the warning issued by the Commission:

> [The higher education industry] has become what, in the business world, would be called a mature enterprise: increasingly risk-averse, at times self-satisfied, and unduly expensive. It is an enterprise that has yet to address the

fundamental issues of how academic programs and institutions must be transformed to serve the changing educational needs of a knowledge economy . . . History is littered with examples of industries that, at their peril, failed to respond to—or even to notice—changes in the world around them, from railroads to steel manufacturers. Without serious self-examination and reform, institutions of higher education risk falling into the same trap, seeing their market share substantially reduced and their services increasingly characterized by obsolescence.[89]

The Commission called on institutions to become "more nimble, more efficient, and more effective" in order to increase the nation's "capacity to compete in the global marketplace" and to provide individuals with "full access to educational opportunities that allow them to be lifelong learners, productive workers, and engaged citizens."[90] Institutions also have a mandate from their most important constituency, students and families. American families continue to view college as a necessary path to a job and increased earnings. Surveys by Public Agenda and Sallie Mae reveal a heightened belief that college is essential for economic well-being and for obtaining employment, as a top priority in deciding to attend college. According to the Sallie Mae survey, 75 percent of students strongly agreed with the statement that college is essential for earnings, and 73 percent strongly agreed that attending college was necessary for their desired occupation.[91]

As an industry, the community college is perhaps best prepared and equipped to respond to present environmental challenges and to the nation's call to action. Stated simply, the paradigmatic shift currently underway in higher education favors community colleges. Over the course of their history, community colleges have transcended industry boundaries by developing systems and practices essential for a segue into a future that will favor nimble, efficient, and innovative organizations.

NOTES

1. Walter Crosby Eells, *The Junior College* (Boston: Houghton Mifflin Company, 1931); Edmund Gleazer, *This Is the Community College* (Boston: Houghton Mifflin Company, 1968); Arthur M. Cohen and Florence Brawer, *The American Community College* (San Francisco: Jossey-Bass, 1982); Thomas Diener, *Growth of An American Invention: A Documentary History of the Junior and Community College Movement* (New York: Greenwood Press, 1986); Steven Brint and Jerome Karabel, *The Diverted Dream: Community Colleges and the Promise of Educational Opportunity in America, 1900–1985* (New York: Oxford University Press, 1989); George A. Baker III, ed., *A Handbook on the Community College in America: Its History, Mission, and Management* (Westport, CT: Greenwood Press, 1994); J. M. Beach, *Gateway to Opportunity: A History of the Community College in the United States* (Sterling: Stylus Publishing, 2010).

2. James L. Ratcliff, "Seven Streams in the Historical Development of the Modern American Community College," in *A Handbook on the Community College in America: Its History, Mission, and Management*, ed. George A. Baker III (Westport, CT: Greenwood Press, 1994), 4.

3. Ratcliff, "Seven Streams in the Historical Development of the Modern American Community College," 6.

4. Ratcliff, "Seven Streams in the Historical Development of the Modern American Community College," 7.

5. Beach, *Gateway to Opportunity*, 13.

6. George B. Vaughan, *The Community College Story*, 3rd ed. (Washington, DC: American Association of Community Colleges, 2006), 27.

7. Beach, *Gateway to Opportunity*, 13.

8. Vaughan, *The Community College Story*, 27.

9. Ratcliff, "Seven Streams in the Historical Development of the Modern American Community College," 11.

10. Beach, *Gateway to Opportunity*, 5.

11. Edmund Gleazer Jr., "Evolution of Junior Colleges into Community Colleges," in *A Handbook on the Community College in America: Its History, Mission, and Management*, ed. George A. Baker III (Westport, CT: Greenwood Press, 1994), 17.

12. Brint and Karabel, *The Diverted Dream*, 34–46.

13. Brint and Karabel, *The Diverted Dream*, 43.

14. Beach, *Gateway to Opportunity*, 12.

15. Brint and Karabel, *The Diverted Dream*, 40–41.

16. Brint and Karabel, *The Diverted Dream*, 42–43.

17. Cohen and Brawer, *The American Community College*, 128.

18. Brint and Karabel, *The Diverted Dream*, 42.

19. Brint and Karabel, *The Diverted Dream*, 11–12.

20. Brint and Karabel, *The Diverted Dream*, 43.

21. Brint and Karabel, *The Diverted Dream*, 62–66.

22. Brint and Karabel, *The Diverted Dream*, 62.

23. Brint and Karabel, *The Diverted Dream*, 58.

24. Brint and Karabel, *The Diverted Dream*, 59.

25. Gleazer Jr., "Evolution of Junior Colleges into Community Colleges," 17.

26. Gleazer Jr., "Evolution of Junior Colleges into Community Colleges," 17.

27. Brint and Karabel, *The Diverted Dream*, 52.

28. Gleazer Jr., "Evolution of Junior Colleges into Community Colleges," 19.

29. Beach, *Gateway to Opportunity*, 14.

30. Brint and Karabel, *The Diverted Dream*, 75.

31. Brint and Karabel, *The Diverted Dream*, 74.

32. Brint and Karabel, *The Diverted Dream*, 73.

33. Brint and Karabel, *The Diverted Dream*, 74.

34. Gleazer Jr., "Evolution of Junior Colleges into Community Colleges," 20.

35. Brint and Karabel, *The Diverted Dream*, 94.

36. Brint and Karabel, *The Diverted Dream*, 94.

37. Carnegie Commission on Higher Education, *The Open-Door Colleges: Policies for Community Colleges* (New York: McGraw-Hill, 1970), 21.

38. Brint and Karabel, *The Diverted Dream*, 133–35.

39. Brint and Karabel, *The Diverted Dream*, 131–35.

40. Brint and Karabel, *The Diverted Dream*, 118–20.

41. Q. J. Bogart, "The Community College Mission," in *A Handbook on the Community College in America: Its History, Mission, and Management*, ed. George A. Baker III (Westport, CT: Greenwood Press, 1994), 61.

42. Center for the Study of Community Colleges, 1978.

43. Secretary of Education's Commission on the Future of Higher Education, *A Test of Leadership: Charting the Future of U.S. Higher Education* (Washington, DC: U.S. Department of Education, September 2006), xi.

44. Gleazer Jr., "Evolution of Junior Colleges into Community Colleges," 27.

45. Gleazer Jr., "Evolution of Junior Colleges into Community Colleges," 22.

46. Brint and Karabel, *The Diverted Dream*, 84.

47. Beach, *Gateway to Opportunity*, 32.

48. Beach, *Gateway to Opportunity*, 34.

49. L. Steven Zwerling, *Second Best: The Crisis of the Community College* (New York: McGraw-Hill Book Co., 1976), xix–xxi.

50. Belkis Suazo deCastro and Melinda Mechur Karp, "A Typology of Community College-Based Partnership Activities" (New York: Community College Research Center, January 2009), 2.

51. U.S. Department of Education, National Center for Education Statistics, Integrated Postsecondary Education, "Table 21. Awards conferred by Title IV institutions, by race/ethnicity, level of award, and gender: United States, academic year 2008–09," http://nces.ed.gov/datalab/tableslibrary/viewtable.aspx?tableid=7105.

52. U.S. Department of Education, National Center for Education Statistics, Integrated Postsecondary Education, "Table 37. Degrees conferred by Title IV institutions, by level of degree and field of study: United States, academic year 2009–10," http://nces.ed.gov/datalab/tableslibrary/viewtable.aspx?tableid=7128.

53. Brint and Karabel, *The Diverted Dream*, 192–94.

54. Alison Felix and Adam Pope, "The Importance of Community Colleges to the Tenth District Economy," *Economic Review* (Third Quarter, 2010): 69–93, http://www.kansascityfed.org/publicat/econrev/pdf/10q3Felix_Pope.pdf.

55. Mindy Feldbaum and Hollyce States, "Going Green: The Vital Role of Community Colleges in Building a Sustainable Future and Green Workforce," National Council for Workforce Education and the Academy for Educational Development, December 12, 2008, http://energycenter.org/index.php/about-us/green-career-network/green-job-resources/398-green-job-reports-a-studies/1583-going-green-the-vital-role-of-community-colleges-in-building-a-sustainable-future-and-green-workforce.

56. Doug Lederman, "State Support Slumps Again," *Inside Higher Education*, January 23, 2012, http://www.insidehighered.com/news/2012/01/23/state-funds-higher-education-fell-76-2011-12.

57. deCastro and Karp, "A Typology of Community College-Based Partnership Activities," 1.

58. deCastro and Karp, "A Typology of Community College-Based Partnership Activities," 14–15.

59. Elaine Allen and Jeff Seaman, "Online Nation: Five Years of Growth in Online Learning" (Needham: Sloan Consortium, 2007), 5, http://sloanconsortium.org/publications/survey/online_nation.

60. Allen and Seaman, "Online Nation: Five Years of Growth in Online Learning."

61. National Center for Education Statistics, Digest of Education Statistics, 2011 Edition, Table 198, http://nces.ed.gov/programs/digest/d11/tables/dt11_198.asp.

62. Pew Research Center, Pew Social and Demographic Trends, "College Enrollment Hits All-Time High, Fueled by Community College Surge, October 29, 2009, 1, http://www.pewsocialtrends.org/2009/10/29/college-enrollment-hits-all-time-high-fueled-by-community-college-surge/.

63. Brint and Karabel, *The Diverted Dream*, 4–5.

64. Zwerling, *Second Best*, 35.

65. Sara Goldrick-Rab, Douglas N. Harris, Christopher Mazzeo, and Gregory Kienzl, "Transforming America's Community Colleges: A Federal Policy Proposal to Expand Opportunity and Promote Economic Prosperity," *Blueprint for American Prosperity* (Washington, DC: Brookings Institution, May 2009), 1.

66. Anthony P. Carnevale and Jeff Strohl, "How Increasing College Access Is Increasing Inequality, and What to Do about It," in *Rewarding Strivers*, ed. Richard D. Kahlenberg (New York: The Century Foundation Press, 2010), 73–74.

67. Secretary of Education's Commission on the Future of Higher Education, *A Test of Leadership: Charting the Future of U.S. Higher Education* (Washington, DC: U.S. Department of Education, September 2006), xi.

68. Secretary of Education's Commission on the Future of Higher Education, *A Test of Leadership*, 1.

69. Richard Arum and Josipa Roksa, *Academically Adrift: Limited Learning on College Campuses* (Chicago: The University of Chicago Press, 2011).), 121.

70. Arum and Roksa, *Academically Adrift*, 34, 40.

71. Laura Fitzpatrick, "Can Community Colleges Save the U.S. Economy?" *Time*, July 20, 2009, http://www.time.com/time/printout/0,8816,1909623,00.html.

72. Goldrick-Rab, Harris, Mazzeo, and Kienzl, "Transforming America's Community Colleges," 3.

73. Goldrick-Rab, Harris, Mazzeo, and Kienzl, "Transforming America's Community Colleges," 12.

74. Sallie Mae, *How America Pays for College 2011: Sallie Mae's National Study of College Students and Parents* (Newark: Sallie Mae, August 2011), 6.

75. Sallie Mae, *How America Pays for College 2011*, 12.

76. Sallie Mae, *How America Pays for College 2011*, 18.

77. Robert C. Dickeson, *Prioritizing Academic Programs and Services: Reallocating Resources to Achieve Strategic Balance* (San Francisco: Jossey-Bass, 2010), 16, 18.

78. Brint and Karabel, *The Diverted Dream*, ix.

79. Kevin Dougherty and Esther Hong, "State Systems of Performance Accountability for Community Colleges: Impacts and Lessons for Policymakers," *Achieving the Dream Policy Brief* (Achieving the Dream and Jobs for the Future, July 2005), 4.

80. Dickeson, *Prioritizing Academic Programs and Services*, 12–13.

81. Secretary of Education's Commission on the Future of Higher Education, *A Test of Leadership*, xi.

82. Secretary of Education's Commission on the Future of Higher Education, *A Test of Leadership*, x.

83. Secretary of Education's Commission on the Future of Higher Education, *A Test of Leadership*, 21.

84. Secretary of Education's Commission on the Future of Higher Education, *A Test of Leadership*, 3–4.

85. Secretary of Education's Commission on the Future of Higher Education, *A Test of Leadership*, 4.

86. Secretary of Education's Commission on the Future of Higher Education, *A Test of Leadership*, 26.

87. Data Points, "2008 Survey of Earned Doctorates," *Chronicle of Higher Education*, January 29, 2010, A4.

88. Jean Johnson and Jon Rochkind, "With Their Whole Lives Ahead of Them: Myths and Realities About Why So Many Students Fail to Finish College," Public Agenda, December 2009, http://www.publicagenda.org/TheirWholeLivesAheadofThem.

89. Secretary of Education's Commission on the Future of Higher Education, *A Test of Leadership*, xiii.

90. Secretary of Education's Commission on the Future of Higher Education, *A Test of Leadership*, xii. Secretary of Education's Commission on the Future of Higher Education, *A Test of Leadership*, 26.

91. Sallie Mae, *How America Pays for College 2011*, 15.

Chapter Two

Paradox of the Present

In this chapter, we move from the past to the present by describing the condition of *paradox* that is a distinguishing feature of community colleges. We can understand the significance of paradox by looking at the landscape of turbulence and unstoppable change in which our colleges operate. Tectonic shifts in the economic, political, social, and technological fabric of American society present community colleges with a challenge never before experienced—simultaneously doing *more* and *better* with *less*. The "more" is the unrelenting demand for access—more service for more people at reasonable cost; the "better" is the pursuit of improved outcomes—particularly completion—in response to accountability mandates; and the "less" is capacity diminished by funding streams that perpetually fall short of institutional needs.

Growing institutions, especially fast-growing institutions, encounter problems with size and complexity that hamper their effectiveness. More of everything—students, programs and services, courses, staff, units and departments, systems, and processes—stretches institutions beyond their operating capacity. This presents a challenge for leaders who are not trained to address simultaneously occurring conditions of growth and reduced capacity. Yet, this is exactly the circumstance in which community college leaders find themselves. They are expected to effectively manage institutions that are inherently paradoxical—colleges in which structure and resources are out of alignment with growth. There is no way out except to find employment in another industry, and for most leaders this is not an option. Besides, most industries are experiencing similar challenges.

In our view, the future is about possibilities or scenarios created by leaders through decisions they make in the present. The decisions that will drive the development of community colleges revolve around contradictory states that collectively contribute to paradox. These states are *growth* and *reduc-*

tion, abundance and *scarcity, continuity* and *change,* and *access* and *completion.* Leaders can choose to resolve the paradox by easing the tension between contradictory states, sustain it by permitting the contradiction to exist, or amplify it by resourcing opposing states. The choices they make in managing contradiction will have much to do with the future shape of community colleges.

WHAT IS PARADOX?

Paradox can be understood as the existence of incongruous states. In modern-day community colleges, paradox is embedded in four sets of simultaneously contradictory conditions: 1) environmental forces at odds with resource needs, 2) cultures embedding contradictory values of abundance and scarcity, 3) organizational architecture misaligned with forces of growth and reduction, and 4) organizational success indexed to access and growth in a public policy context favoring completion and added value. Paradox is generally described as a contradiction inherent in opposing forces seeking resolution. [1] The beauty of paradox, however, is that the contradiction need not be resolved. Rather than changing their mission and structure to align with the external environment, community colleges can draw on organizational attributes perceived as vulnerabilities to foster change and innovation.

For community colleges, paradox is, and always has been, an organizational asset. The idea that success can only be achieved through the resolution of paradox is tantamount to saying that community colleges must relinquish key elements of their mission to eliminate disparities. Consider the following, and ask if your college would be willing to:

- close the open door because resources no longer support growth;
- limit investment in workforce development programs because they divert resources from traditional programs;
- target enrollment to full-time students because they are more likely to complete a degree.

Moves of this type and scale are abhorrent to leaders and staff in community colleges. The notion that paradox cannot and should not be resolved helps us to understand the organizational dynamic that enables community colleges to be creative. They are colleges within a college—microorganizations with simultaneously contradictory purposes embedded in a macroorganization built on shared purpose. For this reason, leaders and staff in this unique organizational entity need to be creative and adaptive. By recognizing that irresolvable tensions exist in the fabric of the institution, they consciously embrace a different understanding of organizational dynamics from that which would be characteristic of conventional management thinking. To perform effectively in a paradoxical organization, leaders and staff must be flexible and improvisational. They must be capable of moving with ease between countervailing states of organizational being, for example, tradition and innovation, competition and collaboration, convergence and divergence, and more.

THE DYNAMIC OF CONTRADICTION

Growth and Reduction

Prior to the onset of the recession in 2008, the future for community colleges was challenging, but at least comprehensible. Now it is an uncharted horizon of contradictory forces. Most colleges are encountering opportunities for growth that are part of a market loaded with learners needing more and better service to find their place in the new economy.

Counterbalancing these opportunities, however, is uncertainty about the resources they will have to support growth and their capacity to absorb growing numbers of learners. The following forces will have a significant impact on how our colleges organize for the future.

Countervailing Forces

Substantive change in the landscape for community colleges can be traced back to 2008 with the onset of the recession and the election of Barack Obama as president. The nation is six years and counting into a recession that has profoundly disrupted every facet of American life. Mobility ground to a sixty-year low in 2010 as unemployment, plunging home values, and declining confidence in the economy forced people to delay major life decisions.[2] Evidence of the difficulty Americans were experiencing with economic uncertainty was everywhere to be seen:

- In reports indicating that the employment decline between October 2007 and April 2010 was the steepest on record since 1945 and that the median U.S. household had lost nearly 39 percent of its net worth from 2007 to 2010[3]
- In surveys like that conducted by Citi with two thousand adults in 2010 indicating that Americans, by more than a two-to-one margin, believed that they were worse off financially than they were the prior year.[4] Some were unguardedly pessimistic about future prospects; for example, 36 percent of the adults surveyed believed the economy had hit bottom, but 59 percent believed economic conditions had not yet bottomed out

- In media articles indicating that the mood of public officials paralleled the plight of citizens as governors in all but a few states indicated that state economies had hit bottom but were not in full recovery, more federal expenditures would be needed to create jobs and spur economic growth, and without renewal, exhausted stimulus funds would lead to further deterioration of public college and university operating budgets in fiscal years 2011 and 2012.[5]

Renewed uncertainty about the health of the debt-ridden global financial system has raised fresh concerns about the prognosis for economic recovery and has signaled the potential for a relapse into recession. In the words of Harvard economist Kenneth Rogoff, "The nation is working through a recession linked to a deep financial crisis—a powerful amplifying mechanism with long-lasting effects. On average, it takes four and a half years to get back to the same per capita GDP where you started out and about the same amount of time for unemployment to stop rising. We haven't yet gotten back to the same per capita GDP where we started. We have never left the recession; we're still very much in it."[6]

The economy showed signs of rebounding in the first quarter of 2011 only to be stymied by slow job growth and the delayed passage of the debt-ceiling legislation. Financial markets turned volatile with the downgrade of the United States' AAA credit rating by Standard & Poor's in August 2011. The downgrade raised borrowing costs for government, business, and consumers. Combined with lingering high unemployment, a widening European debt crisis, and eroding consumer confidence in the economy, its effect was to illustrate the depth of the nation's economic problems. An economy that for the majority of people had been slow growing, but predictable, turned into a roller coaster driven by a political system that could no longer deliver the rising economic performance and living standards the nation had come to expect.

The future is all but certain. The federal debt is projected to grow faster than the nation's annual economic output due to the rising cost of Medicare, Medicaid, and Social Security. Any change in foreign markets will have a ripple effect on the domestic economy. Setbacks are likely, and they will come with little warning and potentially calamitous effect. In the years ahead, the economic landscape will be one of peaks and valleys, with potentially severe implications for public support of community colleges.

Opportunity and Adversity

In every cloud there is a silver lining. Opportunistic investors have long used economic downturns as buying opportunities. Businesses have used the urgency that accompanies slumps to mobilize innovation and renewal. Community colleges have experienced dramatic enrollment gains in periods of economic recession. The current recession is no exception. Enrollment of traditional-age students in community colleges grew significantly between 2006 and 2009. In 2006, 42 percent of traditional-age students enrolled at community colleges, while in 2009, 45 percent did so.[7] Between 2008 and 2009, enrollments of traditional-age first-time students at two-year colleges increased by 8 percent.[8] In 2010, the trend was reversed as enrollment of traditional-age students declined by 5 percent.[9] Multiple factors account for these trends. Growth can be attributed to students who in better economic times might have chosen to attend other (and costlier) types of institutions and those who would have joined the workforce after graduating from high school. Decline can be attributed to capacity strain at community colleges and to early signs of economic recovery.[10]

Opposing forces of growth and reduction can be likened to accelerators and decelerators. As accelerators, they facilitate movement by encouraging change; as decelerators they impede movement by constricting the resources available to institutions. Although virtually all community colleges are working with limited resources, learners do not diminish their expectations. They want more and better service at reasonable cost, and colleges must find ways to deliver or face the consequences. In effect, decelerators become accelerators when leaders must find creative solutions to adversity.

R. L. Alfred described the effect of accelerators and decelerators on community colleges in the following way:

> Accelerators and decelerators make up a dynamic of contradiction that will shape patterns of community college development in the future. On the one hand, if forces of deceleration—a slowly recovering economy, declining resources, and diminished capacity—maintain their grip, enrollment could plateau as institutional capacity falls short of demand. If community colleges choose to deliver more of their core process through temporary staff and lean staffing, nagging questions about quality and accountability could emerge. Learners believing they are paying more and getting less, will invariably push for more, with the result that leaders may have to direct more resources to capacity. Colleges focusing on costs and efficiency and failing to attend to outputs will do so at their own peril in a policy landscape requiring incremental evidence of accountability.[11]

If the economy moves into a sustained recovery, a scenario driven by forces of deceleration is unlikely. In normal times, people return to a pattern of consumption marked by increased spending during a recovery, state treasuries are replenished, and money finds its way into community college operating budgets. These are not normal times, however. As states adopt new revenue and appropriations policies as a hedge against future-year downturns, community colleges will not see a significant influx of new revenue.

They will be forced to cope with the effects of deceleration fueled by a lingering recession and diminished capacity, while simultaneously coping with forces of acceleration fueled by burgeoning learner demand and intensifying calls for accountability. Learners will want more and better service, and policymakers will want evidence of better results.

For institutions and leaders the implication of simultaneous conditions of growth and reduction will be to change or die. Choices will range from hunkering down and working with existing resources to creating new resources through innovation. Hunkering down—which can be likened to a mind-set of scarcity—will place a premium on efficiency and economy. Innovation—a correlate of abundance—will involve creating new resources by changing how we do business. It will mean doing things that were heretofore considered unthinkable: changing the business model, procuring significant private sources of funding, redesigning organizational structures, collaborating with competitors, reengineering culture, streamlining systems and processes, and learning how to change through substitution. The choices leaders make about the contradiction between growth and reduction will have a significant impact on the future of community colleges.

Abundance and Scarcity

Abundance and scarcity are competing mind-sets in virtually all organizations. Some individuals live in a world of scarcity. Their underlying view is that resources and opportunities are limited and must be acquired and protected. The scarcity mind-set is a zero-sum game in which one wins at the expense of another—there is only so much pie to go around, and if one gets more there will be less for another. The fear of loss is a driving motive: losing what one has, losing out on possibilities for getting more, getting less than what one wanted or expected.

Others live in a world of abundance. Their underlying view is that resources and opportunities are unlimited. Opportunities and challenges are to be embraced and pursued. The worst thing one can do is become attached to the status quo because possibilities abound. The abundance mentality involves a win-win orientation—there is plenty for all and we can achieve more together than apart.

Examples abound of how these mind-sets work in community colleges. In the teaching arena, there is the all-too-common scenario of long-serving instructors teaching in the same department with varying degrees of effectiveness. For the purposes of illustration, two instructors begin service at the same time, and through a series of step increases they are pegged on the salary schedule at the same base pay. One instructor views himself as entitled to the position he occupies and the salary he is receiving by virtue of longevity. His performance record is spotty, but he is able to rationalize it as part and parcel of teaching increasingly ill-prepared students. He has paid his dues and has more than earned his share of the limited funds that are available for salary increases. The other instructor has an exemplary performance record and views herself as an eminently skilled teacher. She embraces change as an opportunity to grow and improve and continually encourages colleagues to innovate and bring new ideas to the table. Salary is the least of her concerns, and she is not troubled by salary parity with her colleague. Her focus is on learning and improvement. Both instructors have a place in the institution, but they are working with entirely different mind-sets—one of scarcity and the other of abundance. What will be the contribution of each to institutional performance and vitality?

In the management arena, a similar scenario applies. There is the saga of presidents in neighboring institutions working to reverse an enrollment dip following two years of unprecedented gains. One president is focusing on a short-term marketing strategy to recoup lost enrollment, while the other is developing a long-term strategy to bring new markets to the college. The president with the short-term view believes that first-movers prevail in a market loaded with providers competing for a limited number of students. The president with the long-term view believes that opportunities are abundant, and new markets are always there to be served. The challenge is to identify them and find ways to draw new learners to the college. Both strategies are important. Which is likely to be most effective over the long haul?

Abundance and scarcity are not simply mind-sets at work in organizations. They are cultural values deeply rooted in the American psyche. Americans have historically subscribed to a "psychology of abundance"—a belief that resources and opportunities are plentiful and it is up to each individual to take advantage of them.[12] In the paragraphs that follow, the work of Couloumbis, Ahlstrom, and Weaver is used to describe the evolution of abundance through European settlers who brought with them a profound trust in freedom and individual responsibility and an equally profound distrust of government intervention in any sphere, public or private.[13] This worldview could flourish on a continent with seemingly unlimited natural resources, a temperate climate, and open terrain ripe for settlement. America's isolation from Europe supported its determination to build a new kind of country unburdened by national rivalries and rigid class systems. Individual success was the building block for collective success and reinforced a belief in "rugged individualism." Hard work fueled by values of delayed gratification, frugality, and anticipation of a better future would enable people to move up the economic ladder and, in so doing, promote economic growth.[14]

The American Dream became a reality for most immigrants throughout the nineteenth and into the twentieth century. There were setbacks—the Civil War, World War I, and the Great Depression. Each setback brought a change in orientation with a psychology of scarcity replacing abundance.[15] During the Depression, for example, only the federal government had enough money to stimulate the economy. With unemployment exceeding 25 percent, banks failing, farms and homes being foreclosed, spiraling deflation, and collapsing production, traditional American individualism had to be supported by active government intervention. Franklin Roosevelt's administration had to increase spending to boost demand and create jobs. Once the economic pump was primed, however, the government stepped out of the way, leaving programs in place that stabilized the economy and protected the individual.

The Depression lingered until World War II and gave way to the economic engine that created the consumer economy and launched whole new industries built around new technologies in transportation, telecommunications, electronics, and information. Fueled by readily available consumer credit, efficient manufacturing and distribution, and new goods and services, a psychology of scarcity gave way to abundance.[16] Americans loaded up on goods and services and came to expect continual improvement in life circumstances. The spree came to an end in 2007 with the onset of the worst recession since the Great Depression. A combination of inadequately regulated markets and greed triggered a worldwide economic crisis. American optimism was tempered by the sober reality of grim economic circumstances from which there would be no easy escape. The American psyche once again changed from one of abundance and anticipation of a better future to scarcity and pessimism about the future. Pessimism is a selective emotion, however, as for some the impact of the recession has barely been felt and optimism remains while for others the bottom has dropped out. The upshot is one of simultaneously contradictory mind-sets of abundance and scarcity running side-by-side in a society of haves and have-nots.

For community college leaders and staff, the existence of internal cultures holding simultaneously contradictory values of scarcity and abundance begs the question of how to manage them in the best interests of the institution. At opposite ends of the spectrum are those who view the landscape as loaded with opportunities waiting to be pursued and those who view the landscape as volatile and threatening. One group embraces change, while the other resists it. Between the two groups is a critical mass of people who can tip the balance—those who vary in outlook depending on the issue or circumstance, the behavior of others, and the risk involved. Scarcity and abundance have always been part of the cultural makeup of community colleges. Leaders will continue to struggle with change resisters and adopters. How will they manage them in the organizations that community colleges are in the process of becoming?

Continuity and Change

The third paradox, continuity and change, can be illustrated through the example of three colleges whose structure and systems are at odds with the landscape in which they are operating. The first, Virtuous Community College, has used a formula of open access, low cost, and convenience to drive growth. Growth accelerated during the recession, but conditions changed as the recession eased. Employers intensified their demand for fast-response training programs to prepare workers equipped with superior soft skills—skills that would enable companies to compete on a world stage. A new generation of learners gave voice to an expectation for more and better service—curricula delivering state-of-the-art knowledge through the best technologies available and services customized to individual needs. K–12 schools stated anew a desire for collaboration to break down barriers to learner movement between high school and college. Policymakers intensified their pursuit of accountability by mandating evidence of improved learner outcomes, particularly completion. Virtuous is locked into a command-and-control structure and into operating systems that slow the responsiveness to change. Its systems are inefficient, and communication bottlenecks induced by its hierarchy make fast change difficult. It has reached a point where it must change its business model or risk losing business. Feeling that it really has no choice, the executive team begins the task of changing the business model only to run into resistance from staff satisfied with the status quo. Discretion is the better part of valor, and Virtuous's change agenda is shelved until calm is restored.

The long-serving president of Venerable Community College—a mid-sized institution with a long tradition of service to the community—holds on to an organizational structure long after it has served its purpose, because his power is derived from the structure. Quality staff chooses to leave because opportunities for advancement are limited. Those who cannot leave remain behind and fill key management positions. Competitors sensing vulnerability and opportunity move in and capture market share.

Dualistic Community College chooses to use parallel structures to simultaneously deliver workforce training and traditional academic programs. Instructors teaching in traditional programs want nothing to do with business-oriented noncredit courses. To minimize conflict and avoid the possibility of marginalizing workforce training programs by putting them under the same roof as traditional programs, a parallel delivery structure is formed. This runs contrary to the interests of employers who are calling for laddered curricula to facilitate the movement between noncredit and credit courses. Dualistic is committed to the new structure, however, and fails to make timely changes, thereby losing business to a neighboring college that has restructured its delivery system to meet employer needs.

The problems of these colleges, like those of many community colleges, are rooted in a structure that is not aligned with market dynamics. Market forces shape the growth and development of a college. Yet leaders, in their haste to avoid actions that might impede growth, often overlook critical questions, such as: Where are we now? Where are we going? Is our current structure capable of getting us to where we want to go? Their attention is fixed inward on low-risk adjustments to accommodate growth—tweaking the system rather than making the fundamental changes needed to give the institution new vitality.

Basically these are questions of organizational design—a process of aligning an institution's structure with its mission and vision, and forces in the external environment. There is a saying in architecture that "form follows function." Put another way, the design of a college should support its purpose. Great design means that a college is structured in such a way as to effectively serve its purpose as well as to anticipate and respond to forces in the environment. Poor design is just the opposite. Like a sputtering business, a college doesn't perform well because it has not remained abreast of the needs of its stakeholders, its programs and services no longer meet learner preferences, or it has lost sight of competitors and changing market conditions.

Given the importance of organizational design, why is it given so little attention in community colleges? Why are leaders reluctant to alter the structure of a college to align with market dynamics? The reason is that community colleges as organizations have evolved rather than changed by design. As colleges have grown larger and taken on more functions, management divisions and specialists have been added to carry out the work. With little or no planning and intervention, the organizational structure that has emerged is more often than not misaligned with forces in the external environment. Take the college that has added layers and administrative units to manage growth—a structure that is accompanied by the rigidity, bureaucracy, and communication problems that come with a hierarchical design. Yet the college is operating in an environment of fast-paced change and is expected to turn on a dime to meet constituency needs. It is no longer organized to do so, and institutional performance is compromised as a result.

When one knows what to look for, it is easy to determine when an institution's structure is out of sync with its environment. Imagine a college with academic programs that are coming under intense competitive pressure. The market is changing, and its long-held advantage is eroding. Everyone knows that programs must adapt or die, but much work is involved in redesigning programs to meet market needs. Tweaking the divisional alignment of programs to make them look different is a more attractive alternative than redesigning programs altogether. Accordingly, a decision is made to realign programs among divisions. The new alignment is unveiled at an all-college meeting. Confidence is high. Everyone is on board and committed to the new alignment.

But there is a catch. Beneath the surface-level changes, the old power structure remains. This is a common problem for community colleges at a mature stage of development. "New" structures, whatever their form, are superimposed on old ones. Decision making becomes muddled, and there is a lack of clarity and accountability. New units, which need freedom to operate in a start-up mode, have to work within an existing bureaucracy and established ways of doing things. Leadership teams are often oblivious to these problems until late in the game. Lip service is paid to the new structure, but doubt and frustration run deep, and staff turns to the old structure for guidance and support.

There are good reasons for the misalignment of structure and context in our colleges. Primary among them is a tension between continuity and change. Leaders and staff get stuck in established ways of doing things and have trouble breaking free of the past. The developmental pattern this follows is common within colleges. When a college is in start-up and early growth mode, the leadership team controls core functions. In addition to being responsible for the overall management development of the college, the president is in charge of marketing and external relations and is also the chief fund-raiser. As the institution grows, the leadership team becomes a bottleneck to growth—without help, team members are not able to carry out their roles on a larger scale. So positions are added to cover selected functions—for example, a foundation is established and a director is hired to coordinate fund-raising efforts. At the same time the leadership team is experiencing difficulty in determining how much authority to give up—too much and performance might suffer; too little and they might burn out trying to manage everything.

As the institution develops over time, personnel settle into their roles and ways of operating. The structure evolves organically, and over time leaders and staff grow accustomed to it. The institution operates in a business-as-usual mode, until an opportunity or a crisis materializes and the realization sinks in that success will not be achieved through the current structure. The signs are many—confusion among roles and functions, decision-making bottlenecks, change resisters who get in the way of innovation, or simply slow execution. Regardless of the sign, when inertia begins to dominate and resources cannot be marshaled to pursue opportunity, the structure has outlived its utility.

For community college leaders, the implication of facing simultaneous forces of continuity and change will be one of finding a middle ground that enables structural change while providing the comfort of familiar touchstones. Change is a flexible process that does not need to be either/or—it can be both. It can balance elements of continuity—aspects of current structure

that must remain in place because they are part of an institution's culture—
and elements of change—aspects of a newly created structure, which align an
institution with its environment. Finding an acceptable balance between continuity and change will be one of the foremost challenges facing tomorrow's
community college leaders.

Access and Completion

Balancing agendas of access and completion is perhaps the ultimate expres-
sion of paradox for community colleges. Continuing support of open access
by policymakers has driven demand to a point that community colleges are
altogether different institutions today than they were at the beginning of the
millennium. Meeting increased demand for courses and services using a
business model designed to deliver economies of scale through temporary
staff is part of an uncomfortable truth that threatens to undercut the vitality of
our colleges.

Dimensions of a Paradox

In the short span of a decade, the interests of federal and state governments
and foundations have coalesced to encourage a paradigm shift for community
colleges from one emphasizing access to one emphasizing completion. Because of the open-door mission, this shift and the demand it will place on
institutions and leaders for academic reform has challenging implications. In
Rebalancing the Mission: The Community College Completion Challenge,
Christopher Mullin argues that on one level, the act of gaining access to
college and enrolling constitutes success for all learners.[17] At another level,
however, limited enrollment and course experience is not likely to deliver
significant labor market benefits to the individual. Research has repeatedly
shown that enhanced employment opportunities and increased earnings accrue at each successive level of education an individual attains.[18] Because
growth has always been fundamental to organizational success and keeping
the door open is necessary for growth, community colleges will need to be
creative in responding to the completion mandate. This will invariably mean
a change in business model to reconcile contradictory goals of access and
completion.

Access

Enrollment at community colleges increased almost eightfold from 1963 to
2008 largely because of support from policymakers.[19] Federal actions to
support access included continuing funding for the Pell Grant and other Title
IV student aid programs, aid to institutions serving underrepresented populations, various tax provisions, and judicial decisions that support diversity on

campus.[20] States have improved access by including in master plans a provision for community colleges located within commuting distance of residents, operating and capital appropriations, and policies and actions to assist in preparing K–12 students for college and careers.[21] Support for access continues to come from private foundations such as Atlantic Philanthropies, the Bill & Melinda Gates Foundation, the Ford Foundation, the Charles Stewart Mott Foundation, the Joyce Foundation, the Kresge Foundation, Lumina Foundation for Education, and numerous local, regional, and national foundations dedicated to providing the opportunity for education. Most importantly, access is fueled by institutional policies that declare unwavering commitment to open-door admissions and minimize barriers to entrance and enrollment.

Enrollment and Course Completion

While course enrollment is the first leg of the completion paradigm, it takes institutional effort to keep students enrolled and to see them through to course completion. Community colleges straddle two distinct learner populations—college-age youth and adult learners. This creates opportunities for colleges, but it poses challenges as well. In the realm of opportunity is the potential for growth made possible by admissions policies that welcome all learners. With growth come problems, however, as a significant number of learners entering college are not ready for college-level work. To be successful in college courses, students must have acquired the knowledge and skills provided by a rigorous K–12 learning experience. Yet seven out of ten students leaving high school and entering community colleges need remediation.[22] Working adult learners enrolling in courses to retool knowledge and skills may be at a similar disadvantage because of background experience that is not recent or deep enough to assure academic success.

For these and other reasons, defining success through entry and course completion is incongruent with prevailing views of educational attainment. There is value to completing a course, as the experience of completion is undoubtedly an inducement to enrolling in additional courses and remaining on the path to a degree. Problems come into play, however, when benefit is taken into account: What are the short- and long-term benefits of individual course completion—to the learner, to employers, and to other stakeholders in community colleges? As community colleges focus on improving completion rates, they may need to consider the impact of packaging learning opportunities one course at a time.

Certificate and Degree Completion

Completing coursework to obtain a credential, whether it is a certificate, work-related certification, or a degree, signifies an acquisition of knowledge or skills in a given discipline. The concept of a "credential" opens up a range of possibilities for completion—offering full programs on campus, delivering customized course packages in response to employer needs, making programs and courses available as open courseware to learners on the Internet, and bundling courses in new and different ways to meet changing learner needs. Credentials play an important role in advancing completion, and the manner in which they are configured—broadly or narrowly—undoubtedly has a significant impact on completion.

Given the current economic climate and global basis of competition, there exists growing demand for preparing workers with world-class skills. For community colleges, this demand has manifested itself in growing interest in short-term, work-related education credentials. From 1997 to 2007, there was a 58.4 percent increase in short-term certificates awarded at community colleges as compared to an 18.7 percent increase in associate degrees.[23] The focus on upgrading worker skills through short-term credentials, while necessary and desirable, poses a problem for colleges seeking to increase completion rates in the conventional sense of completion. Institutions and leaders are caught in a conundrum of focusing either on: 1) increasing completion rates using traditional measures (attainment of degrees) established by government agencies for comparative purposes, or 2) upgrading worker skills through industry credentials not counted as a success measure by government agencies. Focusing on the former narrowly defines completion while overlooking the needs and achievements of a significant number of learners, whereas focusing on the latter does little to advance the standing of community colleges with government agencies. Community colleges are therefore in the difficult position of balancing two completion agendas: the need of learners and employers to develop workplace skills and the desire of government agencies to improve performance along a narrowly defined set of outcomes.[24]

COMPETING AGENDAS FOR SUCCESS

Virtually every forecast now points to continuing uncertainty regarding the national economy. There are indications that the years ahead will include intensified global competition, rising costs for entitlement programs, vacillating resources, and restructuring for cost efficiency. In this landscape, community colleges could be permanently weakened by a business model focused on delivering more and better with less. For example, delivering more services through part-time instructors and staff peripheral to the core of the organization has the advantage of stretching scarce resources, but at a cost of reducing service to learner needs. The rationale for "more" is growth—the primary basis upon which success is measured. When one peels away the layers of rationalization for this and other growth-enhancement strategies, however, a question begins to emerge: Who or what is at the center of the quest for success—the institution, students, or something else?

We know that every organization has a natural development cycle; generally there is a period of growth followed by deepening maturity, stability, and then renewal or decline depending on whether a new cycle of growth can be launched. But what if community colleges are so focused on their own success that they cannot envision a road to renewal running through something other than the institution itself? Leaders and staff hold different conceptions of success. Instructors and staff in contact with students in the age of the "customer" worry about having sufficient resources to serve students, but also about making a difference. For them success is embedded in the resources they have to work with and the results of their efforts. Leaders worry about the bottom line—performance. For them success is a matter of organizational change that takes the institution to a higher level of performance whether it be growth, efficiency, student outcomes, or visibility in the public eye. These countervailing views create two problems relative to the agenda for success in community colleges. First, there is not a uniform conception of success shared throughout the institution. Second, and more importantly, there is a means-ends inversion, with the institution becoming the primary focus of success, not the learners who are supposed to be the beneficiary of its efforts.

This conundrum will need to be resolved if community colleges are to develop a business model that will generate a new cycle of renewal and growth. A necessary first step will be to rethink the value equation on which our colleges are built. No longer do they possess the advantage of cost and convenience. The phenomenal advance of distance learning and open courseware, combined with innovations in service delivery to fit changing student needs and interests, have impelled learners to forge new relationships with postsecondary institutions. Colleges that have obscured the interpersonal relationship between teacher and student by focusing on efficiency and cost containment cannot expect to attract and retain learners who expect much more. When learners reconstruct their educational experience in institutions that have made a difference, they acknowledge, above all, not courses or subjects or information and skills imparted, but instructors and staff who changed their lives—people who made a difference in their developing sense of themselves. [25]

Community colleges are now designed for continuity that resists change. This dilemma resides within institutions, and the good news is that it is within their power to remedy. Its basis is structures, processes, and decision-making tendencies that maintain consistency in order to promote stability and growth. Building a college for continuity made sense when people and markets were predictable. But the dramatically accelerated pace of change renders the current business model unfit for optimum performance. To disrupt the development cycle and launch a new wave of renewal and growth, community colleges will need to look deeply into themselves and find ways of managing paradox effectively. The future will belong to institutions and leaders that seek new ways to manage paradox, not resolve it.

THE PARADOX INHERENT IN INNOVATION[26]

In order to manage the paradoxes inherent in their missions and to achieve improved outcomes, community colleges must continue to develop their capacity for identifying and implementing innovation. Yet engaging in innovation is challenging for all organizations. Community colleges, given their unique mission and their relatively short history, have some characteristics that predispose them for innovation. However, they also face unique barriers to innovation, including limited discretionary funds to invest in innovation, lean staffing structures, and numerous regulations and stakeholders to please. This section provides a brief overview of the categories of innovation and the organizational requirements associated with different forms of innovation, followed by a discussion of the leadership and organizational challenges associated with creating and implementing innovations.

Recent literature commonly categorizes innovations as either incremental (also termed *sustaining*) or disruptive (also termed *radical* or *strategic*). Incremental innovations are characterized by targeting existing customers or users by doing more of the same, but better, faster, or cheaper. Disruptive innovations introduce or create products and services that may not initially be as good as currently available products and thus are not initially favored by current customers and users but have features that appeal to new customers and markets. For example, those who would build a better mousetrap do so not by making the current model lighter, stronger, cheaper, and more but rather by changing processes and practices to dramatically improve "trapping a mouse." Improvements may mean using scents or sounds to trap the mouse instead of the traditional cheese and a spring on a wooden board. The new mousetrap would appeal to customers who are "squeamish" about seeing a crushed mouse. Vijay Govindarajan argues that many companies fail to begin "strategic experiments," the precursors to "strategic innovations," until they are already in a state of decline and are forced to, at which time it may be too late.[27] Christensen, who ignited the current ideology embracing disruptive innovation, identified numerous organizations from a wide variety of industries that ultimately failed because their leadership merely followed the strategy of improving the current model of a mousetrap and ignored newly developed, unconventional systems, processes, and practices.

Other theorists have similarly opined that for organizations to succeed in the future, they must embrace disruptive innovation rather than incremental innovation. However, Christensen, Govindarajan, Christopher Trimble, W. K. Smith, and others have also noted that most organizational leaders are more comfortable with incremental improvements rather than radical or disruptive innovation. Govindarajan argued that organizations spend too much time focusing on the front end of innovation (the creative idea generation) and too little time on mastering learning how to implement an innovation.[28]

Smith[29] emphasized that incremental and disruptive innovations "are associated with seemingly competing goals and . . . inconsistent architectures—structures, cultures, processes, and leadership profiles. Innovating involves experimenting, failing and learning, and it is best supported by flat organizational structures with an entrepreneurial culture. In contrast, incrementally improving an existing product involves efficiency and optimization, and is best supported by hierarchical organizational structures and bureaucratic cultures." The contradictory nature of the two forms of innovation also translate into their implementation. The significant and sometimes opposing differences between incremental and disruptive innovation, their effects on the organization, and the different demands of their implementation offer insight into the multivariate nature of the innovation decision confronting the community college executive. The magnitude of the challenge presented by the implementation demands of these different kinds of innovation is illustrated in Table 2.1 by the demonstration of variability in resources and investment required, the timeline of events, definition of "progress," and even the construct in articulating to stakeholders. These elements demonstrate how complicated, and difficult to gauge, the decision can be for the decision maker.

Organizational and Institutional Barriers to Innovation

Colleges and universities are generally recognized to be "mature enterprises," according to the Spellings Report and others. In that respect, they are predisposed to avoiding risk, responding in ways that inhibit trying new ideas or new ways of operating. The danger associated with this stage of an organization's life cycle is that institutions may become complacent, satisfaction with their record of past success deterring the reflection that often precedes successful innovation. In essence, acceptance of the status quo reflects the inherent barriers to innovation adoption that institutions have erected. Thus, a combination of factors including shared governance, academic autonomy, and other characteristics unique to higher education and specifically to community colleges require leaders to navigate through a minefield.

Since higher education is innately conservative and resistant to change, it is not surprising that traditional institutions may buffer themselves against

Table 2.1 Implementation Characteristics for Sustaining vs. Disruptive Innovations

Characteristic	Sustaining	Disruptive
Time Frame/Duration	Short term (weeks or months)	Long term (multiple years)
Predictability of Outcome	Some certainty	Highly uncertain
Rate of Progress	Steady	Sporadic with many stops and starts
Process	Methodical and sequential	Highly nonlinear
Framework	Context-independent	Context-dependent
Paradigm	Mechanistic and targeted	Organic and experimental
Variables	Limited number and small range	Stochastic
Scope	Mainly internal; contained	Exogenous events are critical

the urgency for innovation. Distinguished histories, venerable names, and influential alumni can distance institutions from the call to innovate. Community colleges, however, often do not have these resources; in fact, their mission of serving the community and their open-door admissions policy force them to innovate and adapt to changing needs. Nevertheless, stakeholders with a variety of agendas have been shown to compound the political landscape in which community colleges operate, thereby clouding the relevance of a proposed innovation. These different and often competing agendas can contribute to a dualism of thought in leaders that complicates decision making and may cause leaders to favor one group of stakeholders while alienating another.

Many academic leaders feel that their ability to innovate is constrained by institutional decision processes, which create a substantial barrier. One college leader reportedly quipped, "The world has challenges, but the college has departments. Most issues require integrative thinking that is interdisciplinary and our departments don't allow for that."[30] Academic freedom and the participatory governance structure of community colleges also require special consideration for campus executives engaged in innovation. These policies and practices may result in an unequal distribution of power, resources, and influence within the institution, which could affect the college president's outlook on certain decisions. The shared governance culture necessitates an environment of persuasion, negotiation, and consensus building. Leaders play a broker and mediator role for conflict management and the facilitation of consensus. These roles can add value or, in some cases, further exacerbate the tension for college presidents as they may increase the stakes for the executive charged with innovation decisions, making it more difficult for that person to perform the role while satisfying these other expectations.

There are other factors that may promote resistance to innovation from faculty and staff. Instructors may have concerns about the loss of authority, the lack of transparency in processes, and inconvenient timing. Their perception of being valued and consulted would undoubtedly affect their level of engagement. Reactions from support staff may encompass resources, equal voice, and inclusion. Overall, misalignment between employees and leaders over definitions, expectations, and the dissemination of information within a shared governance context could add complexity to the decision process. The lack of acknowledgement of differential roles, power conditions, and multiple perspectives can contribute to leader's struggles—all of which can be brought to a head when a decision on innovation must be made. All of these elements—organic and integral to the community college environment—make innovation a challenging process and may thwart presidential ambitions in this arena.

The autonomous departmental unit structure of colleges, in which faculty have little impetus for interaction with colleagues from other disciplines, creates a structural barrier to communication and collective understanding of innovation. Segments of the college are insulated from data, performance measures, and other external indicators. Furthermore, faculty rewards and recognition are frequently based on discipline-related work, further deepening a commitment to discipline and the department ahead of the institution. As a result, decision makers feel isolated in their contemplation of the appropriate decision, unsure of support from the faculty ranks.

Administrative hierarchy poses another structural challenge for community college decision makers engaged in managing innovation. When new organizational systems or practices associated with innovation are implemented, it is middle managers who have the most to lose and may become casualties caught between the accountability to leaders for success of an innovation and the responsibility for addressing inertia and resistance of the general population. Yet these are the same people on whom top leaders rely for execution of innovation. College deans, directors, and other midlevel administrators are the "lieutenants" who battle in the trenches for adoption of an innovation. This situation is not lost on college presidents and becomes another consideration in an array of choices related to innovation.

When structures, systems, practices, and culture reinforce one another, leaders may become psychologically resistant to making decisions that disrupt the organization. In the case of institutions where tradition, parochialism, and inertia dominate, the leader understandably may act in a more conservative, risk-averse, and myopic manner. Leaders may lean toward successes of the past (often equated to "consistency") as they prioritize the immediate over the future—a predisposition to incremental rather than disruptive innovation. Fear of conflict, intolerance for risk, and potential loss of confidence can ultimately shape a community college leader's willingness to pursue innovation as well as his/her perception of organizational willingness and readiness for innovation irrespective of the merits of the innovation.

THE PARADOXICAL NATURE OF LEADERSHIP

Community college leaders cannot ignore the call to innovate and are expected to lead their institutions to new horizons. The American Association of Community Colleges' report[31] on competencies for community college leaders highlights the ability to "develop a positive environment that supports innovation" and to "take an entrepreneurial stance" as key tasks for twenty-first-century community college leaders. Higher education has evolved to expect this competency from its leaders. Despite this unceasing and increasingly high-volume call, the decisions related to innovation are not simple: they are complex, ambiguous, and paradoxical. In community colleges, innovation choices are further complicated by academic traditions, staff resistance, and structural barriers.

Progress in innovation is not hampered by a lack of innovative ideas but rather by the inability to make the right decision, especially leadership decisions, relative to specific innovations; to develop the right structure and systems to support implementation; and to foster a culture capable of accountability for results around the core business, as well as the flexibility necessary to deal with the ambiguity associated with a strategic or disruptive innovation in particular. For innovators, the dominant question for which they seek an answer is the "What?" But the more difficult questions (and answers) are why, who, when, where, and how. College leaders must understand the rationale and justification for a specific innovation and be willing to champion the idea. Skeptics and pundits will want to know the benefit and the payoff on investment in innovation. In this environment of scarce resources, it is critical to identify the team to implement the innovation. Is the innovator the appropriate person to lead the team? Can he or she be spared from existing responsibilities? The college president must decide if the timing is right. What is the time frame for the innovation—its development and implementation? Is a pilot program an appropriate approach to introduce the innovation? The identification and recruitment of "early adopters" must also be considered.

Innovation itself promises technological, operational, organizational, and policy advances which, if successful, help leaders to serve the college's mission. The benefits of innovation are real, but equally well known and unsettling are the risks of dysfunctional or failed innovations. Those risks haunt community college leaders who must make decisions on innovation.

They must contend with the knowledge that where risks lead to poor outcomes, the failures often outlast the tenure of the decision maker and may impair the institution they valued or loved. Innovation, by definition, is change, and change is risky.

While many public- and private-sector leaders offer explanations for the difficulties associated with change, researchers point to the constraints on innovation posed by risk-averse leaders who have risen through the ranks based on a specific formula for success. All too often these leaders are confused, uncertain, and conflicted over decisions and actions regarding innovation within their institutions. Community colleges may find it difficult to innovate and fulfill their mission unless their leaders understand and effectively navigate the complexities inherent in innovation.

Moreover, college chancellors and presidents who lead innovation operate in an environment of external as well as internal stressors. Competition from for-profit colleges, greater demands from "consumer-savvy" students, and larger numbers of academically ill-prepared students are source points for escalating pressure on community colleges. Further, participatory governance, public accountability, and academic traditions compound an already complicated situation. Community colleges, and academic institutions in general, are shaped by consensus decision making and diverse stakeholders who commonly produce misalignment of organizational priorities, culture, and resource allocation. Leaders are hesitant, uncertain, and even resistant to dealing with innovation if doing so appears to exacerbate rather than remedy pressure. Until we understand more about what leaders sense and feel as they contemplate innovation, it will be difficult for practitioners to make decisions with confidence and move their institutions forward with authority and assurance.

Ordinarily, leaders who have done well in the conservative environment that is academe have succeeded by avoiding conflict and risk as compared to their counterparts in business. The academic community is well understood to place high value on stability and peaceful coexistence among college constituents and to reward leaders who can maintain those values in campus life. The attachment to stability, essentially the status quo, is reinforced by the leaders' training and experience in education, where long-honored traditions, faculty autonomy, and deliberate, lengthy debates are highly respected. Whereas college chancellors and presidents understand the need for innovation and that formulas do not exist for choosing and implementing the "right" innovation, they tend to hold conventional views that inhibit them from recognizing knowledge and insights from fields outside of education. This disinclination is a contributing factor to inertia and resistance to change. Likewise, social, political, and economic pressures will intensify in the years ahead, and leaders may find it helpful to adjust their sights to decision making in a context of turbulence and constant change.

Vijay Govindarajan, author of *Ten Rules for Strategic Innovators*, espouses that leaders and organizations must invest time and resources in change and innovation:

> As managers run the core business, they develop biases, assumptions, and entrenched mind-sets. These become further embedded in planning processes, performance evaluation systems, organizational structures, and human resource policies. Organizational memory is particularly powerful in companies that tend to promote from within and to have homogeneous cultures, strong socialization mechanisms, and long track records of success. Such deeply rooted memory . . . gets in the way of creation.[32]

Govindarajan also acknowledges that most organizations ably manage incremental change but are "befuddled" by disruptive change. Today's community college leaders focus on a variety of innovations, ranging from online education to granting baccalaureate degrees. However, for most presidents and senior executives, questions arise as to which innovation is the best, which is the best fit for the institution, and what are the consequences of choosing or not choosing a prospective innovation. Theorists and practitioners have reported that decisions about innovations, be they incremental or disruptive, constitute a "situation . . . characterized primarily by uncertainty, ambiguity, and emotionality" for the decision maker.[33]

A hesitant or tepid approach to innovation by leaders may lead to ambivalence, cynicism, and unproductive sentiment among faculty and staff. Blindly following a prescriptive "formula" may be equally detrimental as internal conflict and divisions arise. Innovation is a paradox of choice—to innovate or not innovate, to follow a path of incremental or disruptive innovation, to move forward or stay in place. The choice belongs to leaders and staff working together to design the future of community colleges.

NOTES

1. K. S. Cameron, "Effectiveness as Paradox: Consensus and Conflict in Conceptions of Organizational Effectiveness," *Management Science* 32, no. 5 (May 1986): 545.

2. R. L. Alfred, "The Future of Institutional Effectiveness," *New Directions for Community Colleges*, no. 153 (Spring 2011): 103–12.

3. Megan M. Barker and Adam A. Hadi, U.S. Bureau of Labor Statistics, "Payroll Employment in 2009: Job Losses Continue" (Washington, DC: Department of Labor, 2010).

4. J. Clements, "New Citi Survey: Americans are Mired in Economic Winter Despite Signs of Spring," Citigroup.com, http://blog.citigroup.com/2010/04/new-citi-survey-americans-are-mired-in-economic-winter-despite-signs-of-spring.shtml (accessed August 31, 2012).

5. Alfred, "The Future of Institutional Effectiveness," 106.

6. B. Javetski and T. Koller, "Understanding the Second Great Contraction: An Interview with Kenneth Rogoff," *McKinsey Quarterly*, http://www.mckinseyquarterly.com/Understanding_the_Second_Great_Contraction_An_interview_with_Kenneth_Rogoff_2871 (accessed August 31, 2012).

7. R. L. Alfred, "Navigating Change with a Conventional Organization: Is Your College Abundant?," New Jersey Association of Community College Presidents, plenary presentation, November 9, 2009.

8. E. Hoover, "Recession Reshaped College Enrollment Patterns, but the Sky Didn't Fall," *Chronicle of Higher Education* (July 14, 2011): 1.

9. Hoover, "Recession Reshaped College Enrollment Patterns, but the Sky Didn't Fall," 1.

10. Hoover, "Recession Reshaped College Enrollment Patterns, but the Sky Didn't Fall," 1.

11. R. L. Alfred, "The Future: Mastering the Contradiction," *Community College Journal* 72, no. 3 (December/January 2002): 10–14.

12. T. Couloumbis, B. Ahlstrom, and G. Weaver, "Psychology of Abundance and Scarcity," *Real Clear World* (March 17, 2009), http://www.realclearworld.com/articles/2009/03/psychology_of_abundance_and_sc.html (accessed January 10, 2012).

13. The historical and cultural analysis of abundance and scarcity presented on pages __through__ is based to a significant extent on the work of Couloumbis, Ahlstrom, and Weaver, "Psychology of Abundance and Scarcity."

14. Couloumbis, Ahlstrom, and Weaver, "Psychology of Abundance and Scarcity."

15. Couloumbis, Ahlstrom, and Weaver, "Psychology of Abundance and Scarcity."

16. Couloumbis, Ahlstrom, and Weaver, "Psychology of Abundance and Scarcity."

17. The analysis of policy implications related to access and completion presented on pages __through__is derived from the analytical framework and ideas of Christopher Mullin in "Rebalancing the Mission: The Community College Completion Challenge," *AACC Policy Brief 2010-02PBL* (Washington DC: American Association of Community Colleges).

18. L. Jacobson and C. Mokher, *Pathways to Boosting the Earnings of Low-Income Students by Increasing Their Educational Attainment* (Washington, DC: The Hudson Institute and CAN, January 2009).

19. Mullin, "Rebalancing the Mission: The Community College Completion Challenge."

20. Mullin, "Rebalancing the Mission: The Community College Completion Challenge."

21. Public fiscal support for community colleges has been recorded since 1966 in the Grapevine database, http://www.grapevine.ilstu.edu/historical/index.htm.

22. Bill & Melinda Gates Foundation and Lumina Foundation, Developmental Education Initiative, http://www.deionline.org/.

23. L. Horn and X. Li, *Changes in Postsecondary Awards below the Bachelor's Degree: 1997 to 2007*, Washington, DC: National Center for Education Statistics, Report 2010-167, November 2009.

24. Mullin, "Rebalancing the Mission: The Community College Completion Challenge."

25. D. Noble, "Technology and the Commodification of Higher Education," *Monthly Review* 53, no. 10 (2002): 1–13.

26. Otto Lee, vice chancellor, Instructional Services ND Planning, San Diego Community College District, "Paradox Inherent in Innovation," submitted to the authors June 18, 2012.

27. Vijay Govindarajan and Christopher Trimble, *Ten Rules for Strategic Innovators: From Idea to Execution* (Boston: Harvard Business Review Press, 2005), xxvii.

28. Govindarajan and Trimble, *Ten Rules for Strategic Innovators*, 4.

29. W. K. Smith, "Managing Strategic Contradictions: Top Management Teams Balancing Existing Products and Innovation Simultaneously" (Unpublished doctoral dissertation, Harvard University, 2006).

30. Laura Palmer-Noone, "Perceived Barriers to Innovation: First Report from a Study on Innovation in Higher Education," *Assessment and Accountability Forum* 10, no. 2 (Summer 2000): 3, http://www.intered.com/storage/jiqm/v10n2_noone.pdf.

31. American Association of Community Colleges, "Competencies for Community College Leaders," Brochure (Washington, DC: AACC, 2004), http://www.aacc.nche.edu/Resources/competencies/Pages/default.aspx.

32. Vijay Govindarajan and Chris Trimble, "The CEO's Role in Business Model Reinvention," *Harvard Business Review*, January–February 2011, http://wwsg.com/wp-content/uploads/HBRBusinessInnovation.pdf.

33. Dennis A. Gioia and Kumar Chittipeddi, "Sensemaking and Sensegiving in Strategic Change Initiation," *Strategic Management Journal* 12, no. 6 (1991): 443–48, http://www.qualidadern.org.br/mbc/uploads/biblioteca/1158008033.39A.pdf.

Chapter Three

Organizing for Innovation

Today's community colleges must ask fresh questions of themselves and their various publics, and reconcile these with what they determine as being mission critical or core competencies. A mile-wide and an inch-deep approach to serving the students of the 21st century is an unsustainable enterprise. [1]
—Daniel Phelan, Jackson Community College

A prevailing theme in previous chapters is that the very characteristics that were perceived in previous decades as contradictions or vulnerabilities for community colleges in comparison to their four-year counterparts now constitute fertile ground for innovation. Although resource challenges continue to intensify, community colleges are building capabilities that will put them at the leading edge of a crowded postsecondary market. The idiom "necessity is the mother of invention" aptly describes the efforts of our colleges to redesign themselves for superior performance. Leaders and staff have sharpened their focus on improving organizational infrastructure—from information technology systems, to data collection and reporting, to new organizational models, to customer-focused processes and procedures—in order to achieve greater efficiency and improved outcomes.

This chapter begins with a case study of Onondaga Community College in Upstate New York, which used reaccreditation as a catalyst for systematically reinventing itself over the course of a decade. The case study will be complemented by contributions from prominent community college thinkers who have been asked to speculate on the future of community colleges. These practitioners—presidents and chancellors, foundation leaders, policy and think tank experts, and writers and researchers—add immediacy and diversity of thought in presenting illustrations of new approaches, new tools, and innovative practices for reinventing community colleges.

The changes and innovations highlighted in this chapter have served to leverage the capacity of community colleges to pursue their comprehensive mission in spite of eroding resources, thereby contributing to their equilibrium and vitality. The changes described herein serve as a platform for innovations that will be highlighted in chapter 4 and woven into alternative scenarios for the future development and organizational re-visioning.

A COLLEGE REINVENTED

Onondaga Community College (OCC) in Syracuse, New York, recently celebrated its fiftieth anniversary. No different than its peers, Onondaga's mission, identity, and organizational structure have been largely shaped by prevailing social, political, and economic forces. The college has struggled with many of the same challenges that community colleges across the nation have faced at various points in their development, including enrollment swings, declining public revenues, and mixed levels of public understanding of the college and its mission.

Located in Onondaga County (population 467,026), two miles outside the city of Syracuse (population 145,170), OCC sits in the geographic center of New York State. Its five-county service region, once a thriving manufacturing center, experienced devastating job losses, related population decline, and infrastructure deterioration in the final decades of the twentieth century. In the late 1990s and early twenty-first century, area business leaders, local governments, and civic organizations began to develop coordinated initiatives designed to help Central New York reinvent itself, in part by supporting the growth of the region's knowledge-based industries and entrepreneurial endeavors. A report on "older industrial cities" by the Brookings Institution (*Restoring Prosperity*, 2007) underscored the region's urgent need to shift to a knowledge-based economy through advanced educational attainment by its citizens.[2]

Onondaga Community College realized that it had to play a central role in advancing regional transformation, but in order to do so, it would need to make major changes of its own. During the early 1990s, OCC found itself plagued by unstable enrollment, linked in part to population out-migration, as well as a public image that negatively impacted enrollment. The college, which had been built with a strong academic core, including traditional transfer programs and career-oriented programs, had become insular and out of touch with the changing needs of the community. No different from its peers, Onondaga's fiscal stability depends on stable enrollment, as more than 80 percent of the college's budget is tied to enrollment. In fact, from 2001 to 2005, large-scale enrollment swings began to jeopardize the college's stability. Ultimately, OCC had no choice but to change if it was to continue to fulfill its mission at a time when its success in doing so was more important than ever.

The reaccreditation review process provided Onondaga with an opportunity to reflect on the way in which it was meeting student and community needs. OCC's 1998 self-study portrayed the college as struggling with unstable enrollment and an image problem. It had become complacent in communicating its mission and value to the community, as well as in ensuring that its programs remained accessible and relevant, given the changing needs of current and prospective students and area employers. As a result, Onondaga's Middle States Commission on Higher Education Evaluation team issued the following recommendations:

• As the Onondaga community changes, the college needs to reinvent itself to the extent necessary to meet the needs of a changed society.
• The college should raise the priority of the activities designed to attract new students and retain them once they choose to attend Onondaga Community College.

The Strategic Plan: A Framework for Success

Vijay Govindarajan, professor of International Business at the Tuck School of Business at Dartmouth, argues that all organizations must invest time and resources in three categories of planning: 1) managing the present, 2) selectively forgetting the past, and 3) creating the future.[3] In order to be successful in the present, organizations must be engaged in continuous improvement activities that enhance the quality of existing products and processes, add value, and achieve greater efficiencies. As Govindarajan explains, "Continuous process improvement involves countless small investments in incremental process innovations."[4] But organizations must also be good at strategic innovation, because "through cycles of boom and bust, a fundamental truth endures: change is constant—and often nonlinear. . . . through strategic innovation, corporations cannot only stay ahead of change, they can create change."[5]

At the conclusion of its 1998 self-study, Onondaga began to take charge of its future by establishing a strategic plan designed to enhance the college's capacity to more effectively "manage the present" through continuous improvement and "selective abandonment." Onondaga used the findings that emerged from its 1998 self-study and recommendations of the visiting accreditation team as a call to action. The creation of the college's first strategic plan, *A Framework for Success*, created in 1999, served as the road map for fundamental organizational change and realignment that would be systematically implemented through the leadership of a new president and a supportive board over the course of a decade. Changes included:

- the introduction of strategic enrollment management as a means of stabilizing and optimizing enrollment in order to stabilize finances;
- a research-based brand makeover;
- the renovation and repurposing of physical space in direct support of strategic goals, including enrollment growth and an optimal learning environment;
- the establishment of a new budget development process (plan drives budget) to support strategic goals;
- investment in a robust information technology infrastructure to support existing and redesigned academic and administrative systems and operations;
- reengineered, centralized student recruitment and enrollment services to simplify and streamline processes for prospective and entering students;
- the integration of residence halls and a residential student population, supported by learning communities and reworked food, library, recreational, arts, entertainment, and supplemental programming;
- the development of integrated programming, services, and delivery methods for nontraditional students, including dual credit, accelerated, and online learning;
- the introduction of a new organizational entity—College Affiliated Enterprises—focused on collegewide asset management to produce cost savings and to generate additional revenue.

Strategic Enrollment Management and Student Success

Given the role that enrollment plays in resourcing an institution, building a system for strategic enrollment management became a core initiative in OCC's development efforts. Systems of this type are not viable, however, in the absence of a robust technology infrastructure and information about the alignment of programs and services with community needs, student recruitment and retention, and operating efficiency. OCC invested in technology and beefed up its research and data acquisition capabilities—steps that enabled it to realign and streamline operations to support student recruitment, admissions, and enrollment. This was part of a focused effort to align limited resources with strategic goals by eliminating inefficient functions and processes. To enhance access and strengthen the alignment of programs and services with community needs, a new unit, Corporate and Extended Learning, was created with responsibility for making the college's academic and workforce programs accessible to employers and nontraditional students. This unit was empowered to make changes that would improve the delivery of programs and services at its northern campus (space leased in an old strip mall), enhance existing partnerships and forge new partnerships with area high schools and colleges, close obsolete sites and establish new extension sites, and create online accelerated evening and weekend courses. In preparation for the development and rollout of a strategic enrollment management plan, the college combined fourteen different student enrollment offices and functions into a single, centralized unit for enrollment services, which was eventually named Student Central. This one-stop center was designed to ease student access to enrollment services by improving the efficiency of administrative operations.

Managing Image and Brand

To further refine recruitment and outreach systems, in 2005 OCC conducted extensive research into community needs and perceptions of its brand. It discovered that students had a negative perception of the quality of an Onondaga education *prior* to enrolling at the college—a perception that was dispelled by positive experience once they started classes. It was discovered that prior to attending OCC, students perceived of it as a "last resort," which turned out to be "the first step" for students who, once enrolled, quickly came to the realization that they had made a smart choice. The study revealed a significant gap between students who felt satisfied (66 percent) and those who felt proud (25 percent) to attend Onondaga. As one student commented, "I thought that it was going to be just like high school . . . but to my pleasant surprise . . . the professors are so good and the program that I am in is designed very well."

Onondaga's new credo—Explore, Discover, Transform—emerged from "brand" research. Working with data, OCC leaders and staff moved to close the gap between preconceived notions and actual experience for enrolled and prospective students. OCC's mission and credo were promoted, a new college crest was unveiled, and a comprehensive advertising campaign and new public website were launched. Social media and web-based communications and marketing were dramatically increased as a result of research findings. In keeping with its new brand, the college upgraded the look and content of student and employee web portals to elevate image and to improve the efficiency of campus communications.

Realizing that it could not assume that its branding effort was successful without follow-up data, OCC repeatedly surveyed the community with an eye toward shifts in perception. As shown in figure 3.1, the positive results of its branding effort were evident in the responses to community surveys. Further testimony to the effect of branding was evident in enrollment growth the college experienced after 2004.

After realigning administrative functions to deliver a fully integrated, student-centered enrollment experience and to expand program and service delivery, Onondaga was ready to proceed with strategic enrollment management. A first priority was to attract and retain students by differentiating

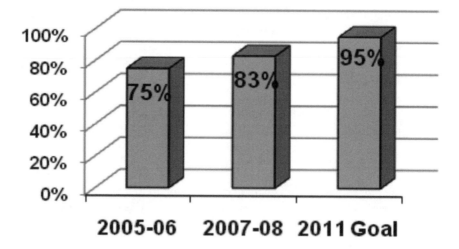

Figure 3.1. Community Perception of Onondaga Community College

OCC from competitors in central New York's crowded postsecondary education market. A number of options were considered, among them an on-campus housing option to attract out-of-area students and to stem the outflow of students from the college's service area. An infrastructure change was required for the campus housing option—a step accomplished by establishing two not-for-profit affiliate corporations adjunct to the OCC Foundation: the Onondaga Community College Housing Development Corporation and the Onondaga Community College Association. These new entities established goals and targeted outcomes aligned with the college's strategic goals and outcomes. As nonprofit organizations, both began building assets that could be invested in high-priority projects in subsequent years.

In 2006, the college opened its first on-campus, apartment-style residence halls, which have operated at full capacity each fall, serving a total of 585 residential students. The launch of student housing directly addressed research that showed that students in Onondaga County were leaving the region to attend colleges that provided a "full college experience." On-campus housing also supported regional efforts to encourage more young people to remain in Central New York after graduating from high school, thereby stemming the "brain drain."

Taken together, the improvement in OCC's image; the rollout of new delivery modes; the redesign of the recruitment, admissions, and enrollment processes; and the physical renewal and expansion of campus facilities helped to reverse enrollment decline and positioned the college to respond to the dramatic growth in demand that most colleges faced as the recession of

2008 hit. By 2007, Onondaga was recognized as one of the fastest growing community colleges in the nation by *Community College Week* and the fastest growing college in the sixty-four-campus State University of New York system. By 2011, Onondaga had experienced a 61 percent increase in enrollment over a ten-year period, making the college one of the fastest-growing community colleges in the nation.[6]

By the time Onondaga approached its ten-year reaccreditation scheduled for 2008, enrollment was booming, and the college's image in the community had literally been transformed. To support continuous improvement and to model its promise of self-discovery, Onondaga decided to use reaccreditation as an opportunity to move beyond mere compliance assessment to ascertaining the degree to which the college was fulfilling its credo; Explore, Discover, Transform. The college adopted the selected topics option to focus on accreditation standards central to its identity and integrity and set out to answer the one fundamental question: Is the college fulfilling its promise of self-discovery to its students, employees, and the community? After hosting several campus forums to initiate the self-study, an overarching theme of integrity and barriers emerged. For students to pursue and achieve success, OCC would need to identify barriers to success, and then execute step-by-step plans to overcome them. Onondaga's self-study was designed to locate barriers and offer recommendations for removing them.

Assessment of student learning and building an institutional culture of assessment emerged as priorities following Onondaga's 2008 reaccreditation process. Continuing to adopt student-centered, one-stop support services, particularly in the college's advisement system, also emerged as a key priority. In addition, Onondaga found itself struggling with the same issues as

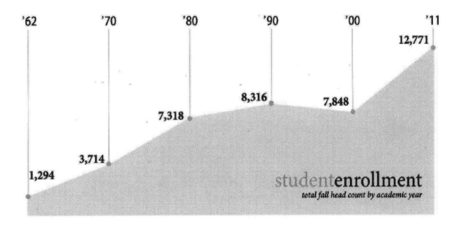

Figure 3.2.   Student Enrollment at Onondaga Community College

many other community colleges—stagnating and declining public funding and stagnant retention and graduation rates.

Funding Continuous Improvement

Throughout the first decade of the twenty-first century, Onondaga was engaged in continuous process improvement on numerous fronts—from enrollment management, to administrative operations, to enhancing the student experience, to improving retention, graduation, and transfer rates. As OCC worked to implement key initiatives focused on increasing student completion rates, the recession beginning in 2007 brought deeper cuts in public funding at the state level and a concomitant decline in local sponsor funding.

In order to combat revenue shortfalls, the college focused on building its capacity to generate new revenue and to achieve operating efficiencies. In 2008 Onondaga publicly launched the largest fund-raising campaign in its history—a $6 million campaign, subsequently increased to a $7.5 million supergoal campaign, to support a new scholarship program, an employee development fund, and capital construction.

In an ongoing effort to push out the brand and simultaneously pursue strategic enrollment management goals, a master plan for athletics was adopted and implemented. The plan included the addition of new sports and new investment to support high-quality athletics that would attract new students. Also, recognizing the revenue-generating power of sports, funding was secured to build a new arena and events center to provide a venue for on-

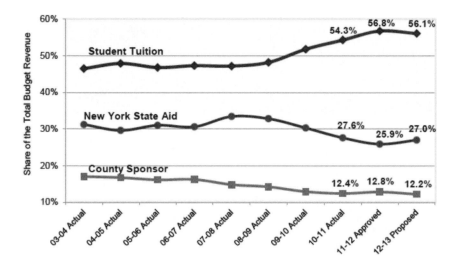

Figure 3.3.   Sources of Revenue for Onondaga Community College

campus events (athletics, arts, and cultural performances) as well as a venue that could be leased to private companies offering programming of interest to the community.

With the capital campaign underway, in 2009 Onondaga's Board of Trustees formed a strategic work group on revenue enhancement charged with identifying strategies and actions the college could take to maximize existing investments and promote revenue growth as the campaign drew to a close. The work group's research resulted in several recommendations, including:

- expanding entrepreneurial initiatives;
- establishing a standard process for faculty and staff to communicate ideas for new entrepreneurial efforts;
- refining the college's financial forecasting model to include expense drivers and to link them to academic programs to inform enrollment planning, resource allocation, and targeted revenue goals;
- adjusting tuition and fees based on real costs, while preserving the mission of access and academic quality;
- continuing newly implemented customized advocacy efforts to support increased investment from state and local sponsors; and
- identifying and amending all policies, procedures, and program requirements that act as disincentives to student graduation, while preserving academic integrity.

In 2010, as Onondaga approached the final year of its strategic planning cycle, it was abundantly clear that the entire higher education industry was facing serious financial challenges resulting from the relentless economic downturn. Against a backdrop of stagnant local funding, and with state funding rolled back ten years to 2000 to 2001 levels, enrollment skyrocketed as more and more students sought the affordable (and now socially acceptable) community college option.

Fortunately, at the same time OCC faced unprecedented challenges to its public funding streams, it had been successful in securing significant local, state, and private investment in technology, campus buildings, and infrastructure. Its nonprofit affiliate corporations had also evolved to a point that they were not only stable but also were poised for future growth. However, these organizations had also grown in complexity to the point that they could no longer continue to rely solely on college staff to manage and oversee their operations.

Selectively Abandoning the Past and Funding Innovation

In *Prioritizing Academic Programs and Services: Reallocating Resources to Achieve Strategic Balance*, Robert Dickeson argues that colleges and universities must not only focus on trying to generate new revenue to maintain the quality of their programs, they must ensure that resources are used more effectively through the prioritization and elimination of programs and services, and the reallocation of resources. [7] He argues that colleges have effectively focused energies on raising revenues—often through student tuition increases that have consistently outpaced the rate of inflation—but have spent too little time systematically working to reduce costs. [8] Of particular concern are the costs of academic programs that have continued to rise because efforts to improve efficiency and to cut costs have tended to focus on the nonacademic side of the house. Consequently most colleges have by default adopted an accretion model, adding programs and increasingly specialized course offerings within programs, without making the difficult decision to streamline or eliminate programs. They thereby create unhealthy internal competition, curriculum creep, and program creep, and they ultimately spread resources increasingly thin. Dickeson states, "Having reviewed hundreds of [strategic plans], it is clear to me that less than 20 percent of them mention where the required resources are going to come from; fewer still identify 'reallocation of existing resources' as a likely source to tap. Strategic plans have become purely additive." [9]

Over the course of the decade, Onondaga worked to increase revenue in support of its strategic goals, as well as to improve efficiency through process improvement, "selective abandonment," and reallocation of resources. For example, in 2002 a previously grant-funded career center was eliminated, with functions dispersed on the basis of demand. And in 2004, the college made the difficult decision to discontinue its dental hygiene program due to cost and quality issues. After years of service to students and the community, and despite extensive efforts in collaboration with the local dental community, the dental hygiene program had become unsustainable, and the college could no longer bear the costs of additional full-time faculty lines required for curricular enhancement. Over time, dozens of obsolete programs and services were eliminated through a well-defined process of program discontinuance.

As with academic program discontinuance, the difficult and contentious process of prioritizing and closing facilities and nonacademic services must be meticulously executed. In 2010, OCC was preparing for a major expansion and renovation of its health and physical education building, which housed a pool used by students and the community. After completing a cost benefit analysis, the college determined that the best way to maximize resources was to close the pool and enter into a partnership with the YMCA to run its fitness facilities and programs, with the proviso that the YMCA would build and operate a modern swimming pool on campus in the near future. In 2011, with the retirement of the college's nurse, OCC conducted a cost benefit analysis of its Health Services unit, and given the availability of four hospitals and numerous health providers within five miles of campus, a decision was made to eliminate Health Services, along with the $20 annual health fee that was charged to students.

The closure of the dental hygiene program and the pool were particularly contentious issues that the college weathered through the resolve of its administration and board. Yet, despite these actions, the tendency to add new instead of replacing the old remained a challenge. As Govindarajan argues, "the forgetting challenge is much more difficult than it may first appear," because the instincts of employees have been developed and reinforced over the years by what has made the company successful in the past. "Structures reinforce old ways of operating, and systems and culture perpetuate the past."[10]

Recognizing the difficulty of simply "managing the present," let alone developing new entrepreneurial initiatives focused on "creating the future," Onondaga again reorganized in 2008 to position itself to fulfill its mission in an era of declining public funding streams. Recognizing that all improvement—academic and nonacademic—must be evidence based, OCC fortified its research function by adding staff and expertise in a newly organized Office of Institutional Planning, Assessment, and Research. Recognizing that tweaking existing structures and systems was no longer sufficient, it developed and implemented a new administrative model, College-Affiliated Enterprises, which was charged with leveraging OCC's assets and nonprofit entities—the Foundation, the Housing Development Corporation, and the Association—to advance its core mission and strategic priorities.

The creation of the College-Affiliated Enterprises division, to be led by a senior vice president whose job was to change habits of thinking and acting to best use campus resources in support of student success, was not just new for OCC. It was new for the higher education industry. The following borrows from Govindarajan's ideas on innovation: "to overcome the forgetting challenge, an organization must have a unique organizational DNA."[11] The establishment of this new division was designed to guide and support the college's efforts to protect its core mission by enhancing existing programs and services, as well as selectively forgetting the past.

At the time, the change elicited a strong response from faculty and staff, many of whom feared that the college was moving to a corporate model and thereby potentially sacrificing its teaching-learning mission at the alter of the bottom line. But the administration, supported by the Board of Trustees, remained focused on the end goal of positioning the college to fulfill its mission in the face of a precipitous decline in public funding. The college was determined that it would not find itself "privatized without a plan," in the words of California University of Pennsylvania president Angelo Armenti Jr., or compelled by inertia toward program closures, retrenchment, enrollment caps, and other draconian measures that were being carried out by colleges across the nation in an effort to balance budgets and remain solvent.[12]

For Onondaga, these changes constituted an important "next step" in establishing the organizational infrastructure needed to support seemingly contradictory goals of reducing expenses and improving quality. Furthermore, they constituted a conscious effort to foster creativity, innovation, and new approaches to teaching, learning, and delivery of service. Not only a learner-centered, assessment-based culture, but a culture of innovation, would be required to overcome challenges the college would face in achieving ambitious goals with funding streams at risk.

Evidence that departments across campus were beginning to think more entrepreneurially began to surface. For example, faced with the need to implement a campuswide emergency broadcasting system, and with cost estimates of several hundred thousand dollars, two departments—Public Safety and Security and Information Technology—collaborated to develop a nonproprietary system using open-source software that would enable the college to broadcast messages to discreet, targeted locations across campus (e.g., a single building, floor, or classroom), or campuswide. The solution required an investment of $30,000 in equipment costs for speakers and equipment to broadcast the messages (a savings of nearly $200,000), and it received recognition from the League of Innovation as a "2011 Innovator of the Year." In an effort to increase sophistication with academic costing models, OCC hired a consulting firm to help calculate the real cost of each of its academic programs. The college's office of Institutional Planning, Assessment, and Research reproduced the reports internally to save costs and enhance OCC's internal planning and assessment capacities.

Continuous Realignment of Resources, Systems, and Outcomes

With the college well on its way to implementing a strategic enrollment management plan and the groundwork in place to support entrepreneurial efforts and to foster a culture of innovation, the final year of the 2006 to 2011 strategic plan was used to establish goals for the 2011 to 2016 planning cycle. The focus would shift from building infrastructure to enhancing learner outcomes—improving graduation and transfer rates, strengthening the pipeline from two-year degrees and certificates to regional career pathways, and improving the financial position of the college by making it less vulnerable to erratic swings in public funding. Learner outcomes are often affected by institutional barriers that prevent students from reaching important milestones. In its new planning cycle, OCC made a concerted effort to remove self-imposed barriers. For example, action was taken to address credit creep by establishing maximum credit caps for all academic programs in keeping with industry guidelines (e.g., sixty credit hours for an associate's degree), thereby saving students time and money. And in accordance with recommendations developed by Complete College America to improve graduation rates and reduce time to completion, Onondaga is advancing initiatives, such as revisions to a long-standing residency requirement, that will make it easier for students transferring from other institutions to count more credits toward an Onondaga degree.

At this juncture, Onondaga continues to implement organization-centered changes, such as a fully integrated budget that includes all 501(c)(3) affiliate corporations, and streamlined processes, practices, and programs—all in support of improved programming and outcomes. For example, in order to address barriers to student success, a single institutional attendance policy is being established; placement testing is being reworked, and developmental programming is being reconsidered and reengineered. A joint faculty-trustee committee with an eye toward more efficient mechanisms (e.g., committees) for practicing shared governance is reviewing the college governance system. Investment is underway in high-functioning, integrated ecosystems—research, innovation, employee performance, assessment of student learning and community needs, enrollment management, and student support systems—to create a foundation for continuous improvement and innovation.

Increasingly, Onondaga is adopting student-centered changes, such as policies to award more experiential credit rather than expecting all students to fit a preestablished mold, designing schedules and support services around student needs rather than staff preferences, and implementing Student Central Phase II—a fully centralized, one-stop student support center designed to deliver a customized, seamless experience for students from the moment they apply until their transition to a four-year college or career entry. These changes will give Onondaga the perspective, agility, and capacity to quickly and effectively respond to the needs of its constituencies. At fifty, Onondaga has not abandoned its access mission. Rather, it has undergone a transformation to preserve and expand its capacity to help students achieve important goals in education, work, and life.

FROM STATIC STRUCTURES TO DYNAMIC SYSTEMS

Onondaga Community College's challenges and approaches mirror those experienced by community colleges across the nation struggling to enhance their capacity to meet accelerating demand in an era of austere resources. The options for doing so are many, but they all boil down to a fundamental reality that no institution can ignore: the need to improve organizational efficiency and efficacy while working to optimize student learning outcomes and program alignment with community needs.

In a 2010 study by the Education Advisory Board entitled "Reengineering the Community College to Meet 21st Century Challenges," community college presidents and chancellors reported a shift in thinking within their organizations toward alternative strategies for everything from delivering instructional material to growing revenue, with the "intention of expanding student access and institutional capacity while leveraging existing resources."[13] If there is one thing that leaders engaged in delivering, funding, writing, or thinking about community college education can agree upon, it is that the core mission extends beyond mere access. The completion agenda encompasses the new and seemingly universal expectation that students who enter a community college will complete academic certificates or degrees and, most importantly, that these credentials will possess real economic value. However, in order to know how best to improve their completion rates, community colleges must (1) have the capacity to identify barriers to completion, only a portion of which are within their influence to remove; (2) be able to develop and implement solutions; and (3) be able to monitor the effectiveness of change and make adjustments as necessary.

National foundations, such as Lumina, the Carnegie Foundation for the Advancement of Teaching, and the Bill & Melinda Gates Foundation have been among the earliest advocates of a college completion agenda. When Lumina launched the Achieving the Dream initiative in 2005 with twenty-seven colleges in five states, the intent was to gather and apply data and research to help improve the retention and success rates of community college students. A 2005 baseline analysis of research on the effectiveness of retention initiatives in community colleges concluded that there is no compelling, research-based evidence to support retention strategies based solely on the student engagement model attributed to Vincent Tinto and commonly practiced at residential colleges.[14] Even though sponsored research suggests that the engagement model, including learning communities, may be relevant in classrooms where students interact meaningfully with faculty and other students, the study concluded that a systems approach is needed. "No program, however well designed, can work in isolation. An excellent developmental or counseling program in a college with generally ineffective teaching may ultimately have no effect on student completion rates."[15] The researchers found virtually no research addressing program institutionalization or collegewide reforms and suggested that given the large number of employed, part-time students, and part-time faculty, significantly improving low completion rates will probably require the successful expansion of pilot programs and the strengthening of related programs and services.[16]

What it comes down to is that the majority of published retention research is written by university-based scholars who have largely overlooked community colleges and their proportionately large population of at-risk students. Bailey and Alfonso contend that most research on effective retention practices at community colleges will likely be carried out within these institutions. Therefore, they recommend that colleges invest more heavily in research by hiring professionals who possess both quantitative and qualitative research skills. They also recommend that colleges and states develop more systematic methods to publicize and disseminate research findings and provide more opportunities for faculty and administrators to discuss evidence about student outcomes as well as to collaborate on solutions.

> The interaction between research and practice should not be seen as a search by experts for the final and definitive answer to the question "What works?" Rather, it is a constant and continuous process—a conversation within and among the colleges and with outside researchers and policy-makers, using the best possible data and the most appropriate methodologies, as practitioners try to improve their practice in a constantly changing environment. [17]

In addition to funding specific initiatives at individual community colleges and compiling results to identify successful strategies, Lumina, the Gates Foundation, and the Carnegie Foundation have helped community colleges develop the infrastructure to identify barriers, forge solutions, and track results—a robust continuous improvement infrastructure that many colleges lacked at the turn of the century. As Jamie P. Merisotis, president and CEO of the Lumina Foundation, advocates below, community colleges cannot merely develop completion goals, they must develop the organizational capacity to support these goals.

> Community colleges are educating more and more Americans—particularly those in the growing populations of 21st century students, including working adults, students of color, low-income students and first-generation college goers. The simple fact is, these students—the ones who used to be called "nontraditional" or "underrepresented" in postsecondary education—now define our future as a nation. For America to prosper economically and thrive socially in the 21st century, we very much need these students—really, all types of students—to succeed in college.

Lumina Foundation's commitment to increasing that success is perhaps best illustrated by their decision in 2004 to launch Achieving the Dream: Community Colleges Count. They have learned a number of important lessons from their involvement in Achieving the Dream, which is now an independent nonprofit organization at work on 160 campuses in thirty states. These lessons, summarized in "Turning the Tide," a recent evaluation report from MDRC, can serve as a vital to-do list for any community college leader who hopes to properly "shape the future" at his or her institution. For example:

• Make sure that student success is truly the central, defining mission at your college.

- Involve the faculty directly and broadly in improvement efforts.
- Emphasize programs that directly affect classroom interactions—those among students and those between students and instructors.
- Emphasize classroom-based measures of learning and metrics that document students' attainment of specific skills, knowledge, and practices.
- Cultivate a culture in which student outcomes data are systematically collected, rigorously analyzed, and—most important—thoughtfully applied to decision making. In short, foster a culture of evidence that is aimed directly at improving student outcomes.

This last example—cultivating a culture of evidence—is hugely important, but it's not something that merely happens. Colleges that exemplify such a culture share several vital attributes, including: multiple senior administrators who are committed to reforms; active institutional research departments; strong leadership and commitment to reforms among faculty and staff; regular evaluation of student-success programs; integrated committee structures that facilitate faculty-administrative-staff communication; and significant investment in professional development.

> All of the lessons listed here underscore a basic truth that applies not only to community colleges, but also to all of higher education. Simply put, the system as a whole must be redefined so that it is far more student-centered and far less institution-focused. The vast diversity among 21st century students demands that we meet them where they are, that we construct programs and processes that help rather than hinder their chances for success. [18]
> —Jamie Merisotis, president and CEO, Lumina Foundation

Developing and implementing effective "analytic ecosystems" is the challenge that Karen Stout, president of Montgomery County Community College in Pennsylvania, has undertaken in an effort to spark "innovation and improvement in pedagogy, student support services, and academic and workforce program development." Describing it as an "organic design," Stout outlines the key components of the analytic ecosystem as:

- a strong mission commitment with significant and consistent Board and presidential leadership, involvement, and investment;
- broad, deep, and inclusive strategic and annual planning systems with outcome-oriented collegewide goals and aligned key performance indicators that reach deep into the organization;
- an organizational structure that values and continually invests in institutional research and information technology coupled with strong systems for organizing data gathering and analysis around macro and micro strategic and annual goals;

- reporting and analysis tools that are deployed to employees at all levels, and to their "desktop," to develop unit-based or course-based "success cards" that enable users to play "what if," with customized data empowering them to make real-time decisions using real-time data;
- systematic and regular training to support employees in using tools, understanding data, and in research methodology and analysis; and
- solid data and technology governance systems to preserve data integrity and data privacy requirements while offering a venue for faculty, staff, administrators, and students to engage in challenging conversations. [19]

According to Stout, "The design, deployment and implementation of this ecosystem will create the type of disequilibrium that is important for keeping our community colleges alive and relevant. . . . "It will be vital for leadership development programs of the future to support new academic leaders in developing this analytical competency." [20]

Analytical leadership was imperative when Tompkins-Cortland Community College (TC3) in Dryden, New York, sustained cuts in public funding that led to the elimination of 9 percent of its employment base, in addition to significant operational cuts. According to TC3 president, Carl Haynes, "As we are confronted with unprecedented budget challenges occurring at a time of ongoing enrollment growth . . . how we structure our various academic and non-academic support services seems vital to how well we will contribute to the success of our students." [21] Through evidence-based restructuring and strategic technology investments, silos at TC3 have "largely dissolved," according to Haynes, who emphasizes, "We no longer use the term 'division' in referring to any of our organizational units since that term is clearly divisive rather than a way of uniting people in their efforts." [22]

Human Capital

In order to significantly improve success rates for the majority of students, new knowledge and skills will be required for leaders and staff responsible for structuring the academic experience. Over the past decade, the number of full-time faculty at community colleges has been in rapid decline as part-timers have become the new faculty majority on most campuses. Also, the American Association of Community Colleges predicts that more than 80 percent of today's community college presidents intend to retire in the next decade. [23] According to Josh Wyner, executive director of Aspen Institute's College Excellence Program, "It is more important than ever that we revisit strategies for recruiting and training people who will lead institutions and teach students, adopting human capital practices aimed squarely at significantly improving student success under 'new normal' conditions." [24] He recommends:

- training professors to access and use real-time data on student success to inform teaching, and community college leaders to use data to align resources with those things that improve student success;
- creating in community colleges the kind of job-embedded professional development opportunities that seem to seriously improve student learning in K–12;
- recruiting leaders who believe that all students can learn and graduate, and developing in them the specific skills needed to lead institutions to much better student outcomes;
- aligning incentives for professors and presidents to the goal of improving student success in ways that avoid negative unintended consequences (such as limiting access).[25]

Like Stout and Haynes, Wyner acknowledges that "pursuing these and other human capital reforms may require re-casting roles, increasing demands on professors and leaders, and, having contentious conversations." The failure to enact structural reforms involving the recruitment, training, and support of true change agents will, according to Wyner, "severely limit the potential of this vital movement to improve community-college student success."[26]

Leveraging Resources and Capacity Building

> Throughout the history and development of community colleges in the United States, the ability to leverage resources has been one of these institutions' greatest strengths. In fact, I would argue that this strength has enabled their continued growth and success.[27]
> —Toni Cleveland, president/CEO, Higher Education Research and Development Institute

Part of the reinvention underway at community colleges involves the adoption of completely new approaches to the way in which institutional resources are leveraged and used in support of student success. For Carl Haynes at Tompkins-Cortland Community College, increasing enrollment concurrent with reductions in public funding presented both a challenge and an opportunity. In the true spirit of problem solving, which so frequently leads to innovation, Haynes and his executive team grappled with how to serve more students with fewer employees while maintaining high-quality performance and learning standards. Their solution was to use the principles defined by the Toyota Production System, sometimes referred to as "Lean Office."

> Using the tools developed by Toyota in identifying and eliminating waste, significant progress was made in a remarkably short time. The staff at TC3 was able to reduce over $70,000 in costs annually by improving their registra-

tion process to the point that no academic manning was required on the day of registration. They also designed and implemented an online catalog that could be accessed by all potential and active students to determine course requirements and staff assignments electronically. The result was an annualized savings of $30,000 in printing and distribution costs associated with paper catalogues.

Another opportunity addressed by TC3 leadership was the reduction of cleaning costs in the Residential Life Department. The former situation was a flawed process that sometimes lost track of which rooms students actually occupied. The existing process frequently resulted in cleaning empty rooms or not identifying responsibility for damage to the dorm. The new process pushed student tracking down the organizational ladder to the appropriate level so the administration knew which rooms were available, and where to spend resources on cleaning and repairs. This resulted in the elimination of duplicated services and unreimbursed repair charges.[28]
—John Kennedy, Hawthorne Consulting

Other initiatives undertaken by Tompkins-Cortland included developing a more consistent and accurate academic information system, resulting in a reduction of last-minute changes and waivers. The college has also designed and implemented an improved document-scanning process that streamlines record keeping, reduces paper storage, and provides better service to students. In using Lean Office principles to control costs and improve student services, Haynes and his colleagues have also noted improvement in employee morale. Employees who are engaged in problem-solving workshops develop ownership of newly designed processes and require less supervision, fewer hours to complete tasks, and greater pride in the work being done. For Tompkins-Cortland, leveraging existing resources more efficiently has reduced costs, improved quality, and elevated morale.

"Reengineering" to meet new demands by altering institutional policies and practices and investing in continuous improvement is exactly what Dan Phelan is tackling at Jackson Community College in Michigan where a values-driven, integrated approach to student success is well underway.

Based upon a review of the literature, related data, as well as the consideration of advancing technologies, constituent behavior, and competition, I concluded some years ago that the days of the "comprehensive community college" were over. Most concerning to me, in the evidence, is the alarming rate in which revenue budgets are principally comprised of tuition and fee revenues—suggesting that higher education is increasingly perceived as a "private good," thereby making the heretofore social contract, invalid.

With the aforementioned as a reasonable premise, we at Jackson Community College, an institution of about 11,500 credit students, have undertaken an intentional approach to advancing a "total commitment to student success" and service excellence among all employees. This approach was undertaken so to distinguish ourselves in the global marketplace on the high ground of quality and student achievement (i.e., our market niche). To that end, the College grafted the Baldrige Criteria for Performance Excellence across all that it does. Its seven elements are incorporated in efforts ranging from board monitoring reports, to balanced scorecards, alternative accreditation, routine benchmarking strategies, budget development, strategic planning, community transparency, and even in meeting structures . . . all in pursuit of institutional and student excellence.[29]

The strategic use of facilities and other assets in new ways is an effective means of expanding institutional capacity. In *Maximizing Value through Program Prioritization*, Dickeson contends that the most likely source of needed resources going forward will be reallocation of existing assets; that is, money, people, time, space, and equipment.[30] Reallocating existing resources can be vexing when space, structures, and assumptions are perceived to be threatened.

Recognizing the potential for capacity building in reprioritizing existing resources, Phelan advised,

Ultimately, in my view, today's community colleges must ask fresh questions of themselves and their various publics, and reconcile these with what they determine as being mission critical or core competencies to their organization.[31]

At Onondaga Community College, all existing resources are being reevaluated and, in many cases, deployed to support multiple functions. For example, space, supplies, and equipment formerly used exclusively by the hospitality/culinary program are now shared with the food service vendor, thereby optimizing the use of assets and generating new revenue to offset academic program costs. Not surprisingly, this unorthodox arrangement presented sundry logistical and scheduling challenges and generated a spirited dialogue about the rightful "ownership" of campus facilities. The "ownership" question is perhaps the easiest one to answer at a publicly funded institution. The more difficult questions are generally procedural in nature, and being mindful of procedural "justice" from the outset is paramount to success. Developing sound methodologies and systems for program analysis and prioritization, and doing so in an environment of transparency, can help to mitigate the angst caused by decisions involving the addition, consolidation, restructuring, reduction, or elimination of programs. In the end, however, angst or no angst, wringing optimal value out of every available asset and reining in the sprawl and expense that has resulted from inertia and program accretion will be necessary as the dual goals of access and success come into sharper focus.

Some colleges, like Ozarks Technical Community College in Springfield, Missouri, and Bunker Hill Community College in Boston, Massachusetts, have gained national media attention for their creativity in leveraging existing resources to respond to new market demands. Ozarks's late-night classes, first offered in the spring of 2010, helped to accommodate student work schedules and filled seats that generally sat empty at night. Similarly, with thirteen thousand students in a facility designed for five thousand and faced with growing demand, Mary Fifield, president of Bunker Hill Community College, describes the pressure of responding to the demands of a diverse student population as the basis for a decision to offer classes at midnight.

> What began as an access issue—constrained by physical limitations—quickly became an opportunity for students. Shift workers, such as airport baggage handlers, police officers, hospital workers and mothers with young children were most prominent among those who populated the first two courses offered: College Writing I and Psychology. Three semesters later, 71 students were enrolled in five different midnight courses. I have concluded that this College's "innovation" may, over time, pale in comparison to grander ideas. The message however is loud and clear. Community colleges are dynamic, turn-on-a-dime, can-do enterprises that believe higher education belongs to everyone . . . anytime and anywhere. [32]

Developing and Testing Approaches to Support Completion

> Today we accept the necessity to finish what we start by focusing on completion as well as access. [33]
> —Jack Becherer, president, Rock Valley College

Community colleges across the nation are beginning to set ambitious goals for improving completion rates, and they are developing targeted initiatives to identify and mitigate barriers to persistence and completion. Responding directly to President Obama's American Graduation Initiative, Anne Arundel Community College in Arnold, Maryland, recently launched Student Success 2020. The goal, according to ACC's president, Martha Smith, is to double the number of degrees, certificates, and workforce credentials by 2020. [34]

For Audrey Levy, president of Lone Star College-Cy Fair in Texas, a proverbial turning of the table is afoot as Cy-Fair searches for new ways to meet the changing needs of students by shifting from a one-size-fits-all approach to a customized model. As Levy explains, "It has been noted that education is one of the industries that is slow to change. In the past, postsecondary education has taken the stance that we have what the student needs and thus the student has to adapt to the educational environment." [35] Levy attributes major advances in technology, particularly communication technologies, as the fundamental force that has put students in the driver's seat, forcing colleges to accommodate their needs. "We now find ourselves in the position of having to find more innovative means of dispersing information, sharing content, and attracting and retaining students . . . the roles are now reversed. We are now being called on to reinvent ourselves for today's students." Miami Dade College in Miami, Florida, is also rethinking student success, according to Eduardo J. Padrón.

> Student completion is at the top of everyone's priority list today. President Obama has challenged the nation to once again lead the world in the percentage of college graduates, legislators in every state house are demanding accountability for student success, and educators from K–12 through higher education are feeling the heat.

> But success demands a realistic, clear-eyed appraisal of the challenge. Without question, it is a monumental one and to think otherwise is a recipe for falling far short of the goal. One of the most alarming statistics in recent years qualifies the challenge: In the nation's 50 largest urban/metro regions, only 51 percent of students gain a high school diploma, compared to a graduation rate of 80 percent in the late 1960s. Many who do attend college today are underprepared—53 percent nationally and much higher at most urban institutions. Add poverty to the challenge and the scope intensifies. At MDC 46 percent of students live in poverty and 67 percent are low-income.

> We can succeed, but our approach implies a transformation of our institutions. Our institutional silos, beginning with student services and faculty, must dissolve into a holistic and integrated approach. Our interventions must be intrusive and early, utilizing the best of technology alongside personal contact. The right to fail is no longer a valid construct. Learning outcomes must be clearly delineated and assessment of student learning must provide real evidence of the effectiveness of our efforts. Our aim should be to craft a learning environment that sets high expectations, demands responsibility of students as well as faculty and staff, and provides unprecedented support for students. And then, persistence, unlimited persistence, should ensure student success.

> Our completion efforts are now characterized under the rubric of MDC's 3 Cs approach: commitment, community and completion. For students, commitment implies the development of qualities that underlie academic success, including perseverance and resilience, accountability, and a willingness to engage with members of a learning community. For faculty and staff, the commitment is certainly to excellence, but beyond that, to a willingness to endure the uncertainty of change and to participate in finding new ways to craft the learning environment.

> Community may very well imply the dramatic reorganization of the institution. MDC's Honor's College is a prime example of a group of students, faculty and support personnel banding together in support of each person's learning. Such a strategy is a rather monumental challenge for an institution

with 174,000 students. But combining technology and personal connections, we believe a new era of collaboration among all the participants in our community is possible. The key to scaling may rest in our application of technology. Imagine for a moment a model that considers the academic and personal challenges that each student brings to the College's doorstep, and then forecasts or preempts the difficulties students encounter. Our support for students could then be specific and begin at the door.

Completion is the fundamental benchmark for students, faculty and staff. But for all concerned it must mean that deep and lasting learning has occurred. Ironically, completion should imply a beginning, should mean that each student has exited the institution not only with a specialty degree in hand, but also with the internal designation of being a learner, one who has embraced that lifelong asset.[36]
—Eduardo J. Padrón, president, Miami Dade College

The Dallas County Community College District, Texas, is responding to the state's priority of access and success by implementing a districtwide strategic retention initiative. DCCC chancellor Wright L. Lassiter Jr. says a $2.5 million investment "aided the seven colleges of the District to identify, develop and implement student success and retention initiatives designed to assist students in reaching their higher education goals."[37] It also funded the establishment of a District Office of Student Retention to work with the colleges to facilitate retention efforts across the district. Lassiter says, "The plan includes adopting the tenets of Achieving the Dream, the Colleges Count program, and most recently the Completion by Design program funded by the Bill & Melinda Gates Foundation." DCCC is one of five institutions that constitutes a cohort of Texas colleges to develop a student success model for all community colleges in Texas. Funding creativity is part of the plan, as Lassiter explains:

The retention initiative has also provided the opportunity for our colleges to be creative, innovative, and risk-taking in implementing strategies and interventions to assist students who are first-generation, minorities, under-prepared and low-income. Funds provided for this program have assisted in the identification of barriers to success for students. Twenty-nine different programs and projects were funded and provided instructional and student support services at the seven colleges. A major project in this program is the African American & Latino Male Initiative. This program was launched in 2009 and now consists of clear steps that have created a culture of success among minority males, and empowered over 500 male students to achieve academic success and to remain in college.[38]

Valencia College in Florida has adopted a comprehensive approach to student support as a primary strategy to improve completion rates. Today's community college students face many of the same challenges that community colleges face—competing demands on their time and attention and financial resources that threaten their ability to succeed. Just as the challenges facing community colleges make resource allocation planning all the more critical to success, the challenges facing community college students require them to commit to, and plan for, completion. As Valencia president Sanford Shugart explains:

> As the community college movement focuses more attention on the challenge of degree completion, Valencia has recognized that getting students to care more deeply about degree completion may contribute more powerfully to results than any other initiative. Beginning a decade ago, the college created a model of student engagement called LifeMap to move students forward by identifying and making a connection to a direction as early as possible in their college careers. This included efforts to encourage every student to develop, as early as possible in his experience at Valencia, a plan to graduate.[39]

Rethinking What Works in Developmental Education

Given that academically underprepared students make up an increasingly large proportion of community college enrollment and the fact that most students who enter developmental courses never emerge with a degree, there are numerous efforts underway to tackle the proverbial elephant in the room. A recent Jobs for the Future report concluded that "a significant redesign of remedial education—how it is organized, delivered, and taught—is required if the nation's community colleges are to achieve more than incremental progress in increasing student success."[40]

At San Jacinto College North in Houston, Texas, additional full-time instructors have been hired who are dedicated and trained in developmental education. Student support services such as cost-free, face-to-face and online tutoring have been added, and the college has implemented mandatory student orientation and intentional academic advising programs. San Jacinto North's president, Allatia Harris, claims that "the cost of various success initiatives can be sustained by retaining developmental students until they achieve their goals of certificate and degree completion or university transfer." Harris says that becoming an Achieving the Dream college "added momentum to a variety of initiatives" in the following ways:

- administrative efforts have kept class sizes at an optimum level for student learning with investments in dedicated learning spaces;
- the college has expanded professional development programming for faculty, including routinely sending faculty to the Kellogg Institute for training; and

- curriculum changes have included course redesigns in math, reading, and writing, as well as the development of a mandatory student success course.[41]

Course redesign is gaining momentum as a promising solution to the developmental problem. In a project designed to improve student success in mathematics, the Carnegie Foundation for the Advancement of Teaching is working to connect research and practice. In partnership with a network comprised of teams from twenty-seven community colleges in eight states and three four-year institutions, as well as research and design partners, Carnegie is developing new pathways to success for non-STEM majors by replacing the current mathematics sequence and course content with a compressed sequence that enables students to "move to and through a college credit course in one year."[42]

New Pathways in Developmental Education

Anthony Byrk advocates the integration of research and practice as a success solution.

Community colleges are gateway institutions for many Americans and second-chance institutions for countless others, enrolling almost half the nation's undergraduates. As is the case in other sectors of education, but especially in community colleges, student access isn't a problem as much as student success.

A complex set of sub-problems operating within community colleges contribute to the reasons students are not able to progress toward a degree, certificate or transfer. Instructional systems do not engage student interest in learning; student support systems inconsistently meet students' needs; human resource practices and governance structures create barriers for change; and there is insufficient access to data and insufficient use of data to inform improvements. Small gains may be possible by focusing on single elements, but dramatic change ultimately requires a systems view of how these elements (and others) inter-lock to create the overall outcomes currently observed.

What is needed in community colleges and in all of education is a new approach to the complex problems of educational improvement where the work of "research" and "practice" join. This approach invites scholars to engage in applied R&D, but in quite different ways in the pursuit of a science of improvement. Carnegie is applying this approach to address the alarmingly high failure rate of community college students in developmental mathematics.

In partnership with a network of college teams and design and research partners, we are developing two new pathways that jettison the current mathematics sequence and course content and replace it with a more compressed sequence that allows students to move to and through a college credit course in one year. These pathways, Statway™ and Quantway™, introduce the mathematics that will help students understand the world around them that non-STEM majors might need. They provide extra support from faculty, tutors and advisors who can help students succeed in math, even if they have struggled in the past. We are collaborating with 27 community colleges in eight states and three, four-year institutions.

Carnegie has created Networked Improvement Communities (NIC) to develop these two pathways. These NICs engage the community college faculty who teach and implement the pathways with Carnegie's improvement specialists and researchers to test hypotheses, analyze local adaptations, and over time contribute to the modification of the pathways. The NICs also include institutional researchers who are working together to build common evidence systems to enable the network to measure, compare and improve the performance of students both within and across institutions. The deans and administrators from each college are addressing the multitude of logistical issues that arise in embedding an innovative design within their institutional contexts. The work of these teams is supported, in turn, by expert others.

As these pilot efforts proceed, the network will address concerns around faculty development and where and how technology can add value. The network will form a robust information infrastructure to inform continuous improvement. It must consider how issues of literacy and language mediate mathematics learning, and scrutinize how the vast array of extant academic, social, psychological/counseling services can be better integrated to advance student success. These are all key to advancing efficacious outcomes reliably at scale.

Taken together, this assembled expertise provides the initiating social form for our NIC, which we call a Collaboratory. As the network evolves, Collaboratory membership will expand to other specialized practitioners, design-developers and researchers as new needs and priorities come into focus.

As initiator for the network and support for the Hub (the formal body that tends to the health and well being of the network itself), Carnegie is orchestrating a common knowledge development and management system to guide network activity, and make certain that whatever we build and learn becomes a resource to others as these efforts grow to scale.

Faculty are at the center of this network improvement system, leading from practice to advance measurable improvements in student success. We believe that this approach will not only produce powerful solutions to the challenges of developmental mathematics, but will also offer a prototype of a new infrastructure for research and development. Carnegie's aim is to support system reforms that will simultaneously impact community college instruction, the field of developmental mathematics and the process of continuous educational improvement.[43]

—Anthony Byrk, president, Carnegie Foundation for the Advancement of Teaching

In a report about how six states—Connecticut, Florida, North Carolina, Ohio, Texas, and Virginia—are organizing to improve outcomes in developmental education, Michael Collins suggests that states are emerging as the most logical and efficient locus of support for the type of broad and deep innovation underway at the Carnegie Foundation.[44] Through policies and capacity-building efforts that identify promising practices, certify student outcomes, and disseminate proven models quickly and effectively, states can effect systemic change. A vehicle for the work of states is the Developmental Education Initiative launched in 2009 by Manpower Development Corporation (MDC), a nonprofit economic and workforce development organization in North Carolina.

Like community colleges across America, Virginia's 23 institutions are required today to do more with less. This challenge, however, describes more than just our finances. Along with the Obama Administration's call for an additional five million college graduates, our governor is calling for an additional 100,000 Virginia graduates. These calls conflict with two dynamics in Virginia. The first is that half of all recent high school graduates are unprepared for college-level work and need developmental education. The second is that the state's population surge is fueled largely by families with little or no higher education experience.

To help resolve that conflict, Virginia's Community Colleges must improve on developmental education success rates. A bold, dramatic comprehensive reform of our developmental education offerings is at the heart of our work to reengineer and improve what our colleges do. We are changing the way we identify and remedy student weaknesses. We are realigning our mathematics requirements, ensuring they are appropriate to an individual's credential and career pursuit. We are doing this across the entire state with a priority placed on transparency. In short, we are summoning the spirit of innovation that first created our community college system nearly half a century ago to confront Virginia's unmet higher education needs.

Committed to advancing state policy efforts initiated by the first cohort of Achieving the Dream partners, the Developmental Education Initiative states, including Virginia, will work to strengthen and scale up promising strategies for increasing the persistence and success of students who start college in need of remedial coursework. These states are in the early stages of testing and implementing strategies to accelerate the identification, implementation, and scale-up of new approaches, e.g., expanding innovations in curriculum, acceleration, institutional policies, and student services to help more students move more quickly into credit courses.[45]
—Glenn Dubois, chancellor, Virginia Community Colleges

Strengths-Based Student Development

The Center for American Progress proposes a "re-imagining" of basic skills education that is student-centered. "A new approach to basic skills education in community colleges would be one that sees development not through a deficit model, but as an opportunity for growth and preparation."[46] Given the overwhelmingly strong correlation between socioeconomic circumstances and educational attainment, the proposed new model would require assessments that link scholastic readiness with measures of student economic self-sufficiency and knowledge of financial aid options. Maps to goal completion would include the recognition of barriers and individual challenges, such as demanding work schedules, lack of computer access, family problems, and more. Hybrid courses would be offered that enable students to garner college-level content while building basic skills, and student portfolios would be used extensively for the assessment of learning. The Center for American Progress also proposes:

- a redesigned and standardized assessment process that incorporates outreach and interventions in the elementary-secondary system, along with summer academies;
- an approach that recognizes the unique needs of adults returning to college after breaks in the educational process;
- semester-based, classroom-centered skills development courses replaced by learning modules, self-paced programs, and learning communities—virtually and face-to-face.[47]

College-to-College Alignment

Beyond changes within colleges and strengthened secondary to postsecondary alignment, the completion agenda requires strengthened intracollege connections. Some believe that the simple practice of accepting a presenting credential—a high school diploma, a certificate, or an associate degree—as a no-strings-attached passport to the next level may be part of the solution. SUNY chancellor Nancy Zimpher describes student mobility as paramount to student success, arguing that "community colleges should work together and closely with universities to ensure ease of transfer—that students' credits carry, that coursework and programs are as relevant and portable as possible between and among schools."[48] The public is increasingly wary of the wasteful duplication and redundancy that has become pervasive in the secondary and postsecondary continuum. Likewise, the Center for American Progress emphasizes the need for better alignment between community colleges and four-year institutions.

The Direct Connect program in Florida presents a promising model for college-to-college alignment, as does the Jack Kent Cooke Foundation Community College Transfer Initiative. Both initiatives seek to advance what Zimpher refers to as student mobility. According to E. Ann McGee, president of Seminole State College in Florida, "With most 21st century jobs requiring credentials beyond a high school diploma, and with funding for education on the decline," the University of Central Florida and four Florida College System partners—Brevard Community College, Lake-Sumter Community College, Seminole State College, and Valencia College—signed a joint resolution in 2005 establishing DirectConnect.[49] A line from that resolution reads: "Day-to-day collaboration among partner institutions will provide a climate for planning, trust, and innovation, capturing best practices and the most creative thinking from each partner."[50]

> The college has squarely faced the fact that the Associate of Arts degree has little intrinsic value in the workplace and even in navigating through the system of higher education. It is not required for transfer to most universities, nor for any kind of employment. Students perceive little advantage in earning the degree and more typically choose to accumulate credit hours in courses they do perceive to have value. In short, the college understands that it is a bridge, not a destination . . . [DirectConnect] has established a clear value for students to earn the Associate of Arts degree. This has been accomplished by a board to board agreement that makes the associate degree a requirement for transfer to our only large, public university in the region and, even more importantly, guarantees every Valencia graduate full acceptance to the highly selective UCF and treatment as a native student for any competitive upper division programs.[51]
> —Sanford Shugart, president, Valencia College

Anne Kress, president of Monroe Community College (MCC) in Rochester, New York, believes that community colleges must function as a lightning rod for college-to-college alignment. "Much like the now-proverbial hologram in which each part contains all of the information possessed by the whole: each corner of a community college contains an innovation designed to disrupt historical barriers to higher education access."[52]

The Community College Transfer Initiative (CCTI) funded by the Jack Kent Cooke Foundation supports college-to-college alignment by incentivizing eight highly selective colleges and universities to increase their enrollment of high-achieving, low-to-moderate income community college transfer students. According to Kress, over the 2006 to 2010 CCTI funding cycle, more than two-thirds (68 percent) of MCC students applying to Cornell University were admitted.[53] In comparison, Cornell's regular admittance rate over the same time was less than 25 percent, and its transfer admittance rate was less than 33 percent.[54]

Significantly, MCC's creation of what became known as the "Pathway to Success" with Cornell University led to even greater opportunities with other highly selective colleges and universities—without the incentive of external funding. Monroe Community College now has similar articulation agreements in place with Amherst College, Columbia University, Mount Holyoke College, Smith College, University of Michigan, and University of North Carolina-Chapel Hill. Unfortunately, without the access and—in very real terms—intervention of a community college, the students now looking at much brighter futures because of this program would likely never have had such horizons. As one recent MCC transfer/Cornell graduate observed, "Five years ago I was working on a construction site . . . and I saw no reason that would change," and in a vote of confidence for the work that goes on in the educational sector that launched him, he added, "I would hope that I will be able to pursue an interesting career, perhaps even be able to teach at a community college." Another reports that she would like to "make some radical changes to America's education system and bless others with the opportunities that I've been blessed with." Christensen notes in his work on disruptive innovation that new entrants into these formerly closed markets "nearly always win." The stories of MCC students granted access to highly selective colleges and universities underscore this observation: they have won, and they want others to have the chance to win, too. [55]

—Ann Kress, president, Monroe Community College

COMMUNITY COLLEGES: PATHWAYS TO CAREER OPPORTUNITY

An important driver of the demand for improved completion rates is the growing demand among employers for an increasingly educated workforce. Not only must community colleges prepare workers who can help businesses compete on a world stage, they must also collaborate with communities in economic recovery and revitalization. Nancy Zimpher, chancellor of the State University of New York, emphasizes the increasingly important role community colleges play in workforce development.

> Over the past few decades, driven by developing technologies and the commensurate requirement for a highly specialized, knowledge-driven workforce, community colleges in New York have evolved to meet new needs—all while maintaining their original mission to provide universal access to higher education by removing economic, social, and geographic barriers. [56]

There is a distinct sense of urgency as agencies of federal and state government and corporations sharpen their focus on the growing gap between the large number of skilled, credentialed workers needed to keep companies and the nation competitive and the relatively low number of college graduates. Changing demographics add to the challenge and the urgency.

With a focus on innovation as part of the solution, the Bill & Melinda Gates Foundation has established a goal of doubling the number of low-income adults who earn postsecondary degrees or credentials by age twenty-six. The foundation is focused on ensuring that a high school education results in college readiness and that postsecondary education results in a degree or certificate with genuine economic value. Its strategy focuses on stimulating institutional practices focused on completion while decreasing the time and cost required to complete a credential that has value in the workplace. Gates Foundation investments have been directed to innovations in performance management and institutional practices that enable more students to get through credential-granting programs. Among these innovations are incentives reinforcing the motivation to succeed, alliances providing new and more efficient on-ramps to postsecondary education, and practices bridging the preparation gap and keeping the focus on completion.[57]

Partnering to achieve shared, strategic goals is perhaps one of the community college sector's most common means of leveraging resources. Donald Snyder, president of Lehigh Carbon Community College in Pennsylvania, contends that "community colleges provide the common link to bring all sectors of society together to build a nation of learners equipped with the key skills and education to succeed."[58] The Lehigh Valley Career Pathways program links Lehigh Carbon Community College, sponsoring Lehigh County school districts, the Lehigh Career and Technical Institute, the Workforce Investment Board, and employers and industry together as partners toward the goal of advancing college readiness and establishing career direction for regional youth.[59]

Linda Thor, chancellor of the Foothill-De Anza Community College District in California, is building partnerships and pathways to establish a Science Learning Institute intended to become a national model for STEM education with the goal of increasing the number of students completing STEM degrees by 25 percent.

> It represents an intentional transition to active, project-based learning and inquiry-based instruction that illuminates synergies among disciplines. It will use "living laboratories" in the community and on campus, including Foothill's large capital investment in solar power and energy management systems. Leveraging Silicon Valley relationships, faculty members are expanding partnerships for research, instruction and internships with industry, NASA and world-class universities to bring STEM careers alive for students. Outside experts are advising on biotechnology, sustainable/energy engineering, computer science, nanotechnology and multidisciplinary programs. Foothill's Science Learning Institute builds on a strong foundation to meet regional workforce needs, increase student access to STEM careers and enhance institutional capacity.[60]

At the new College of Western Idaho (CWI), Berton Glandon, president, has established partnerships with business and industry to deliver fast-track and customized training that "quickly provides knowledge and skills to the workforce of the region" and builds the enrollment needed to maintain a strong fiscal position. By securing donations of equipment and assistance in developing industry-recognized programs and employment for its graduates, CWI has formed a strategic alliance with employers who rely heavily on its graduates to achieve their business goals.[61] It's the kind of win-win scenario that James Catanzaro, president of Chattanooga State Community College in Tennessee, describes as a "transforming strategy for community colleges, particularly in jurisdictions focused on economic development through corporate recruitment and expansion." According to Catanzaro, effective strategic training partnerships yield new revenue, esteem, and connections for the college; the acquisition of cutting-edge facilities and equipment; and the credibility and market advantage that comes with certificates and degrees that lead directly to jobs.[62]

It is this credential-to-job link that Brian Bosworth, president of FutureWorks, believes to be most critical. Bosworth presents a compelling case for expanding the number and range of occupational certificate programs, like those that the College of Western Idaho and Chattanooga State Community College are delivering through strategic alliances with business and industry.

> The United States faces an imminent decline in the education attainment of the labor force that will constrain economic growth and limit national prosperity.
>
> Over the next several decades, the labor force will not grow at anywhere near the rate of growth of the past several decades when the baby boomers reached working age. But, slow labor force growth is only half the story. We can expect virtually no gain in the educational attainment of the workforce, at least as a consequence of young adults moving into and through the labor force. The older cohorts in the current labor force (from age 35 to 54) are now as well educated as the younger cohorts (age 25 to 34), especially in the percentage with at least a high school degree, but also in the percentage with some postsecondary attainment. There can be no more "automatic" attainment gain as current workers age and older workers leave the labor force. In fact, without some big changes in the pattern of attainment by age, race, and economic status, it is likely that the newer workers coming into the workforce will have lower levels of attainment than the older workers leaving.
>
> We will not be able to halt this looming decline unless significantly higher percentages of working adults and low-income and minority youth complete college credentials with labor market value. These groups are not finding success in conventional degree pathways at anywhere near the level required.

We almost certainly will not come close to ambitious national attainment objectives without a very large and very rapid expansion of non-degree credentials—specifically, sub-baccalaureate certificates awarded for completion of carefully organized, occupationally focused programs of study of at least one academic year in duration.

This is a big challenge to postsecondary education but there is good news here.

First, careful review of labor market research indicates that most certificates of one year or more have significant value in the labor market (while those of less than one year generally do not). Second, it seems feasible to quickly ramp up certificate programs; some community colleges in some states are showing the way, boosting enrollment in these programs and producing large numbers of quality certificates. Third, there is evidence that completion rates in some of the best, most rigorous certificate programs are significantly higher than in degree offerings. Fourth, there is evidence to suggest that certificate programming can be economically efficient both for students and for state and federal higher education investors. Finally, there are strong indications that low-income and minority youth and working adults can find in certificate programs the success that has been so elusive in degree programs.

This is not an argument that low-income and minority youth and working adults should be "tracked" into certificate programs rather than into degree programs where long-term economic and social returns may be greater (for the relatively few who manage to complete them). Good certificate programs are stepping-stones to further degreed education, not a dead-end alternative to it.

However, they are also stepping-stones to good jobs.

In the contemporary economy, where some form of postsecondary credential is increasingly the ticket of entry to family-supporting jobs, America's inverse pyramid of sub-baccalaureate education that produces half as many associate's degrees as bachelor's and half as many one-year-or-more certificates as associate's degrees makes little sense. A national commitment to expand high quality certificate programs of at least one year offers a strategy to reverse the likely decline in labor force educational attainment, meet postsecondary attainment objectives, serve hard-to-serve populations, and strengthen economic growth.[63]

SUMMING UP

The changes and innovations described throughout this chapter have leveraged the capacity of community colleges to enhance and perform their mission in spite of declining resources. More importantly, they have primed community colleges for disruptive innovation—a performance arena that will distinguish more from less successful institutions, and this is our subject in the next chapter.

NOTES

1. Daniel J. Phelan (president, Jackson Community College), excerpted from an untitled essay submitted to the authors, August 4, 2011.

2. Jennifer S. Vey, *Restoring Prosperity: The State Role in Revitalizing America's Older Industrial Cities* (Washington, DC: The Brookings Institution Metropolitan Policy Program, 2007).

3. Vijay Govindarajan and Chris Trimble, "The CEO's Role in Business Model Reinvention," *Harvard Business Review*, January–February 2011, http://wwsg.com/wp-content/uploads/HBRBusinessInnovation.pdf.

4. Vijay Govindarajan and Chris Trimble, *Ten Rules for Strategic Innovators: From Idea to Execution* (Boston: Harvard Business Review Press, 2005), xxi.

5. Govindarajan and Trimble, *Ten Rules for Strategic Innovators*, xxv.

6. Onondaga Community College enrollment data provided by Onondaga Community College.

7. Robert Dickeson, *Prioritizing Academic Programs and Services: Reallocating Resources to Achieve Strategic Balance* (San Francisco: Jossey-Bass, 2010), 20.

8. Dickeson, *Prioritizing Academic Programs and Services*, 20.

9. Dickeson, *Prioritizing Academic Programs and Services*, 22.

10. Govindarajan and Trimble, *Ten Rules for Strategic Innovators*, 26.

11. Govindarajan and Trimble, *Ten Rules for Strategic Innovators*, 10, 47.

12. Angelo Armeti Jr., "Lacking Enough State Support," *Chronicle of Higher Education* LV, no. 10 (October 31, 2008), http://chronicle.com.

13. Education Advisory Board, "Reengineering the Community College to Meet 21st Century Challenges," 2010.

14. Thomas R. Bailey and Mariana Alfonso, "Paths to Persistence: An Analysis of Research on Program Effectiveness at Community Colleges," *Lumina Foundation for Education New Agenda Series* 6, no. 1 (2005): 2–4, 11.

15. Bailey and Alfonso, "Paths to Persistence," 21.

16. Bailey and Alfonso, "Paths to Persistence," 21.

17. Bailey and Alfonso, "Paths to Persistence," 14.

18. Jamie P. Merisotis (president and CEO, Lumina Foundation), excerpted from an untitled essay submitted to the authors, July 28, 2011.

19. Karen Stout (president, Montgomery County Community College), excerpted from an essay "Building Analytic Capacity," submitted to the authors, July 28, 2011.

20. Karen Stout, "Building Analytic Capacity," 2011.

21. Carl Haynes (president, Tompkins-Cortland Community College), excerpted from an untitled essay submitted to the authors, July 29, 2011.

22. Haynes, untitled essay, July 29, 2011.

23. Marilyn J. Amey and Kim E. VanDerLinden, "Career Paths for Community College Leaders," *American Association of Community Colleges Leadership Series* no. 2 (2002), http://www.aacc.nche.edu/Publications/Briefs/Pages/rb062420022.aspx.

24. Josh Wyner (executive director, Aspen Institute's College Excellence program), excerpted from an untitled essay submitted to the authors July 26, 2011. Wyner notes that the term *new normal* was a term used by Daniel Yankelovich to describe the challenges facing higher education in "College Presidents Are Too Complacent," *Chronicle of Higher Education*, May 15, 2011.

25. Wyner, untitled essay.

26. Wyner, untitled essay.

27. Toni Cleveland (president and CEO, Higher Education Research and Development Institute), excerpted from an essay "Leveraging Resources," submitted to the authors July 29, 2011.

28. John Kennedy, Hawthorne Consulting (project for Carl Haynes at Tompkins-Cortland Community College), excerpted from an untitled essay submitted to the authors August 9, 2011.

29. Daniel J. Phelan, untitled essay, August 4, 2011.

30. Dickeson, *Prioritizing Academic Programs and Services*, 24.

31. Phelan, untitled essay, August 4, 2011.

32. Mary Fifield (president, Bunker Hill Community College), excerpted from an untitled essay submitted to the authors, August 29, 2011.

33. Jack Becherer (president, Rock Valley College), excerpted from an untitled essay submitted to the authors, August 10, 2011.

34. Martha A. Smith (president, Ann Arundel Community College), excerpted from an untitled essay submitted to the authors, July 26, 2011.

35. Audrey Levy (president, Lone Star College-Cy Fair), excerpted from an essay "Walk a Mile in Their Shoes," submitted to the authors July 28, 2011.

36. Eduardo Padrón (president, Miami Dade College), excerpted from an essay "Rethinking Student Success," submitted to the authors August 3, 2011.

37. Wright L. Lassiter (chancellor, Dallas County Community College District), excerpted from an essay "The Dallas County Community College District Retention Initiative," submitted to the authors July 29, 2011.

38. Lassiter, "The Dallas County Community College District Retention Initiative."

39. Sanford C. Shugart (president, Valencia Community College), excerpted from an essay "DirectConnect—A Disruptive Innovation between Valencia Community College and the University of Central Florida," submitted to the authors August 8, 2011.

40. Michael L. Collins, "Driving Innovation: How Six States Are Organizing to Improve Outcomes in Developmental Education," JobsfortheFuture.com, April 2011, http://www.jff.org/publications/education/driving-innovation-how-six-states-are-or/1218.

41. Allatia Harris (president, San Jacinto North), excerpted from an untitled essay submitted to the authors September 9, 2011.

42. Anthony S. Byrk (president, Carnegie Foundation for the Advancement of Teaching), excerpted from an essay, "A New Approach for Student Success," submitted to the authors August 1, 2011.

43. Anthony S. Byrk, "A New Approach for Student Success," August 1, 2011.

44. Michael Collins, *Driving Innovation*, 2011.

45. Glenn Dubois (chancellor, Virginia Community College System), excerpt from an untitled essay submitted to the authors August 12, 2011.

46. Brian Pusser and John Levin, "Re-imagining Community Colleges in the 21st Century: A Student-Centered Approach to Higher Education," Center for American Progress, December 2009, 44, http://www.americanprogress.org/issues/labor/report/2009/12/08/7083/re-imagining-community-colleges-in-the-21st-century/.

47. Pusser and Levin, "Re-imagining Community Colleges in the 21st Century," 43.

48. Nancy Zimpher (chancellor, State University of New York), excerpted from an essay "Community Colleges' Critical Role in Building a Vital 21st Centure Workforce," submitted to the authors August 12, 2011.

49. E. Ann McGee (president, Seminole State College), excerpted from an essay "Direct Connect: A Higher Education Partnership That Is So Much More Than 2 Plus 2," submitted to the authors August 1, 2001.

50. McGee, "DirectConnect."

51. Shugart, "DirectConnect."

52. Anne M. Kress (president, Monroe Community College), excerpted from an essay "Pathway to Success: A Partnership between Monroe Community College and Cornell University to Promote Transfer of Underrepresented Students," submitted to the authors August 31, 2011.

53. Kress, "Pathway to Success."

54. Kress, "Pathway to Success."

55. Kress, "Pathway to Success."

56. Nancy Zimpher, "Community Colleges' Critical Role."

57. Bryan Cook and Terry W. Hartle, "Why Graduation Rates Matter—and Why They Don't," *Presidency* 14, no. 2 (American Council on Education, 2011, Spring/Summer): 4.

58. Donald Snyder (president, Lehigh Carbon Community College), excerpted from an untitled essay submitted to the authors July 27, 2011.

59.   Linda Thor (chancellor, Foothill-De Anza Community College District), excerpted from an untitled essay submitted to the authors July 27, 2011.

60.   Thor, untitled essay.

61.   Berton Glandon (president, College of Western Idaho), excerpted from an untitled essay submitted to the authors June 24, 2011.

62.   James L. Catanzaro (president, Chattanooga State Community College), excerpted from "The Impact of Corporate Partnerships," submitted to the authors July 10, 2011.

63.   Brian Bosworth (president, FutureWorks), excerpted from an essay "A Quick Case for Expanding Occupational Certificate Programs," submitted to the authors August 29, 2011.

Chapter Four

Shape of the Future

Lumina has always recognized the nation's community colleges as innovators,
and innovation is certainly imperative now. We believe community colleges
can and must play a central role in redefining American higher education.
—Jamie Merisotis, Lumina Foundation [1]

Over the course of a century, community colleges have transformed the
higher-education landscape by dramatically expanding access to postsecondary education. During their early years, our colleges didn't have to work to
be innovative. Their very existence was an innovation. As education "start-
ups" unencumbered by linear business models and the traditional culture,
staffing models, and systems of four-year institutions, community colleges
expanded the definition of who colleges serve, and how, by blurring the lines
between secondary, postsecondary, and career and applied education and
training.

As illustrated in the previous chapter, today community colleges are as
focused on improving student completion rates as they are on preserving
access. New initiatives to improve student engagement, retention, and outcomes are beginning to take hold. From reengineering student intake and
enrollment, to redesigning developmental education, to expanding partnerships with four-year colleges and employers, change initiatives are both
promising and laden with challenges. If not fully resourced, they may prove
insufficient to the task of maintaining access and improving completion.

In *Ten Rules for Strategic Innovators: From Idea to Execution*, Govindarajan outlines four kinds of innovation through which organizations attempt to
revitalize their existence: continuous process improvement (small investment
in incremental process innovation), process revolution (major leaps in improvement of existing business processes through implementation of new
technologies), new product and service launches (new products/services that

do not alter established business models), and strategic innovations (innovations in process or product that involve unproven business models).[2] Strategic innovation is particularly important for organizations that face significant barriers to growth due to capacity constraints inherent in an existing business model when coupled with changing environmental conditions. Organizations that have reached a growth plateau risk entering a period of decline if a new strategic innovation, and consequently a new "life cycle" for the organization, is not launched. Govindarajan cautions that organizations often forego focusing attention on strategic innovation until they "hit the growth wall and performance begins to suffer." Yet it is precisely through strategic innovation that organizations "create change."[3]

Community colleges may ultimately find it necessary to create new systems and new models to effectively deliver instruction and support services in an increasingly competitive global marketplace. Some of the models being developed and deployed today present opportunities to transform the learning experience for students and the credentialing systems available to colleges and universities. Made possible by new technologies, these models transform the learning experience by offering radically new ways of answering three fundamental questions of strategy that define the current "business" model of higher education: *who we serve*, *the value offered*, and *the delivery method.*[4]

STREAMLINING CHOICE AND FLOW

Community colleges have helped to redefine who the higher education industry serves by making college widely accessible to individuals, regardless of background, ability, or income. They have presented a new value proposition and used new delivery methods. They have expanded access by offering a wide array of options to an increasingly diverse learner population, including working adults. Yet, as community colleges work to build and rebuild programs, structures, and systems that support student success, due consideration should be given to limiting rather than expanding choice. "Choice" can mean many things. Used here we refer to "an abundance or variety of alternatives from which to choose." Consider, for example, the array of programs, curricula, and course options available to students from which they can choose. Research shows that students can be overwhelmed by too many options. Institutional policies and procedures, such as providing students with numerous options for majors and course selection, can negatively impact retention and graduation rates and *may* be a contributing factor to the statistic that more than 20 percent (thirty-seven million) of the working adult population has started college but not completed a degree.[5]

Complete College America president Stan Jones argues that environmental shifts, in particular growth in the number of students completing degrees part time while working, combined with the shifts in college policies and practices including a proliferation of choice in courses available, have been united to create a maze of unlimited and poorly defined educational pathways that have morphed from a positive attribute expanding educational access into a barrier for increasingly time-strapped students juggling numerous pressures and competing responsibilities.[6] Many colleges are simply not set up to meet the needs of "the new majority" of students, and thus they cannot break away from their completion rate plateau. Jones argues that colleges should provide more predictability and structure and reduce the time it takes for a student to graduate. He challenges community college boards to "seize the moment and help leverage this crisis by fixing things long broken, removing archaic obstacles to student success, and reinventing American higher education."[7]

At American colleges, our good intentions have paved a road to extended periods of "self-discovery," course catalogs the size of phone books, and chaotic schedules poorly matched to the needs of today's students. Our education values encourage us to want more time, more choice, and more flexibility. But it turns out that the path we're on is actually an expressway over a cliff: America has dropped from first place to 12th in the world in college attainment. Today, only about half of those who pursue a four-year degree full-time finish it within six years. Worse yet, little more than two in 10 students pursuing an associate degree full-time make it to graduation day in three years.

Leading the world again in college completion requires that we open our eyes to the changing nature of today's college students—and how we educate them. Today, the "traditional" college student balances work with education. According to a recent study by Public Agenda, nearly half of students at four-year colleges work more than twenty hours a week. These numbers are even greater at community colleges, where 60 percent of students are at jobs more than twenty hours a week, and a quarter are working over thirty-five hours. But at almost all colleges, courses are scheduled all over the weekly calendar. To speak to the needs of today's students, courses should be structured every day, five days a week, from 8 a.m. to 2 p.m. With this move, full-time attendance would be possible for many more students, significantly shortening the time it takes to graduate.

Private colleges tend to be more flexible and accommodating of student schedules and needs, but changing policies isn't about public versus private colleges. Nor is it just about college students. It's also about the human capacity to process an abundance of choices. In one study, subjects became nearly paralyzed when presented with twenty-four choices of fruit jams. While 60 percent helped themselves to samples, only 3 percent could ever decide which jam to buy. By reducing the choices to six, nearly a third of the 40 percent who sampled the jams made a purchase.

When our best intentions lead us to consider new legislation and policies designed to increase college graduation rates, leaders must apply these vital tests: Will it reduce the time it takes to graduate? Will it help direct students in making an informed, transparent choice, clearly consistent with their aspirations? Will it provide more predictability and structure in order to ease their daily struggles to balance school and jobs?

Whether choosing jams or college courses, people succeed most when their choices are streamlined and directed. By thinking differently about choice, community colleges can meet the needs of more of today's students and share in the success that comes with more graduates. [8]

As Jones and Robert Dickeson note, it is easy for colleges to add programs and courses in response to demand, but it is much more difficult to streamline choices in order to facilitate completion. Although community colleges are taking early steps in this direction, a "start up" college at the City University of New York has designed itself around the concept of completion—a limited number of programs to select from, a requirement to study full time, and a condensed schedule.

The New Community College (NCC) of the City University of New York, scheduled to open in 2012, will operate from the outset with retention and completion strategies based on research. [9] Its mission is to provide students, especially those underserved in higher education, with a solid academic foundation to persist in and complete programs of study, with a degree leading to workforce entry or a baccalaureate program. With the goal of "moving students toward completion of associate degrees much faster and at far higher percentages than is typical of community colleges in the city and the nation" and "in a way that can be replicated by other colleges," the New Community College will begin with a limited number of targeted degree programs (five) and a requirement that students attend full time and attend a summer bridge program their first year. [10] It will tailor its policies and operating procedures in accord with the circumstances of its students (e.g., accelerated studies) and it will operationalize many aspects of the reimagined basic skills model developed by the Center for American Progress, including simultaneous college and remedial coursework and the use of e-portfolios as a means for assessing learning outcomes. Other key features are as follows:

- Precollege programs and recruitment will include group sessions and support for completion of the Free Application for Federal Student Aid (FAFSA).
- All students will be part of an integrated first-year core curriculum that will take a different approach to developmental skills and required coursework.

- Integrated academic and student services will support academic progress and the timely attainment of degrees.
- Student advisement will be central, and each program of study will present well-defined pathways to degree, transfer, and/or employment. [11]

According to Scott Evenbeck, founding president of New Community College: "CUNY's community colleges, supported by the University's Central Office of Academic Affairs, have been incubators of innovation for some time. Kingsborough Community College led the way with learning communities; LaGuardia Community College is a national leader in the use of e-portfolios; and ASAP (Accelerated Study in Associate Programs), at each of the six community colleges, is demonstrating that it is possible to support our students in the timely attainment of their degrees." [12]

Based on these promising practices and results, the New Community College Initiative was launched by Chancellor Matthew Goldstein in 2008. It is meant to address both the need for a second community college in Manhattan, where enrollments at all CUNY campuses continue to expand, and to build a new model for a community college with a singular focus on student success. The New Community College of The City University of New York is on schedule to greet its first student in summer 2012 with the following vision:

> Founded in the CUNY tradition of access to excellence, the New Community College will support student success in a dynamic and inclusive learning environment. As a public, urban college, we will be recognized for the commitment of our students, faculty, staff, and graduates to their communities and to a thriving, sustainable New York City.

> The overarching goal for the NCC, developed through an intensive planning process that included consultation within the CUNY community and nationwide, is to improve student learning, performance, retention and graduation rates so that students can move on to a job, baccalaureate studies or both in a timely fashion. The NCC strives to increase the number of students who complete their degrees, particularly those low-income, first-generation students from populations traditionally underserved in higher education who enter college in need of remediation. The NCC 3-year graduation rate is 35 percent.

> At NCC the recruitment and admission processes will include group and individual information sessions, so that the decision to attend the NCC will be both informed and intentional. Students will attend a 3-week, 4-day per week Summer Bridge program, after which they will move through the first year and beyond in extensive learning communities shaped by the belief that an alternative model of required credit-based coursework for all first-year students will significantly improve student academic performance. Literacy skills and essential student services will be integrated into college-level courses that will introduce academic and practical learning about professions related to the

programs of study. Full-time attendance will be required for the first-year. The signature component of the first year core curriculum is the City Seminar, which will include reading and writing, quantitative reasoning, and case study topics for project-based learning centered on New York City and designed to build upon students' existing knowledge and commitments. This approach will engage students in constructing knowledge as they tackle big issues in a coordinated curriculum melding developmental work as appropriate for all students. Also part of the first year are Ethnographies of Work courses that will build on students' commitment to employment upon graduation. Instructional faculty will be supported in teams that will include advisors and student peer mentors working together to support student learning. Students will also enroll in a Statistics course in their first year with extended time on task. This common curriculum and the courses in the majors will be linked with co-curricular programming of experiential education and capstone courses. Student work will be presented and assessed through e-portfolios.

The practices that structure the NCC model, including its integrated high impact approach to student success have been well documented by research. Our strong commitment to transparent assessment and program evaluation will produce results that we hope will inform the work of other community colleges within CUNY and across the nation. As Chancellor Goldstein has said, "This is indeed a rare opportunity to build a new college, our first at CUNY in more than four decades, and a new educational model in a national spotlight that will bring our work to the attention of a wide audience. I can think of no more urgent task than to find ways to help more of our community college students succeed in earning their degrees."[13]

Similar to New Community College, the Tennessee Technology Centers (TTCs) are designed around a curriculum that is more highly structured than traditional community colleges. Focused on career preparation, the curricula offered by Tennessee Technology Centers are organized around the goal of successful completion and entry into a specific job field. Unlike other community colleges in the state, the TTCs use a competency-based curriculum. Rather than credit hours and seat time, programs follow a clock-hour format in which faculty and students work together over the course of the semester. This structure allows for self-paced learning and allows students to progress at a rate corresponding to the competencies they build.

With a highly focused mission, the TTCs have been able to develop programs that are closely aligned with knowledge and skills in demand in targeted career pathways and that provide students with opportunities to build and demonstrate competencies forged around completion. According to a report by Complete College America, the five-year completion rate for first-time, full-time students at TTCs ranges from 62 to 94 percent, compared to a range of 6 to 13 percent at other community colleges in the state.[14] In 2008, the gap in completion rate between TTCs and Tennessee community colleges was nearly 60 percentage points. Job placement rates are also comparatively high, with the majority of graduates earning salaries above entry level for the region.

ALTERING DELIVERY METHOD

Colleges and universities have quickened the pace of new technology adoption in student and administrative services and operations, but the same cannot be said of instruction and course delivery. As described by Jeff Selingo in an editorial in *The Chronicle of Higher Education*, "The core of the academic experience for students today is almost exactly the same as it was for their parents decades ago . . . on most college campuses we still have professors at the front of a room or a table with an average of 16 students in front of them."[15]

Western Governors University (WGU) represents a stark departure from this trend. The university was founded in 1995 by a group of governors who were disillusioned by the exponential growth in the cost of higher education combined with a perception that traditional colleges and universities were not adequately meeting the changing needs of working adults and employers. At a meeting of the Western Governors Association, the governors decided to create a university that would be governed by member states. Among its unique attributes, the governors determined that the university would maintain a commitment to being responsive to employer and societal needs, cost-effectiveness, and the use of online learning technologies to allow students to progress based on "competencies rather than seat time."[16] The Western Interstate Commission on Higher Education (WICHE) and the National Center for Higher Education Management Systems (NCHEMS) helped to design the nonprofit university, which began accepting students in 1999.

WGU is accredited by the Distance Education and Training Council (DETC) and the Northwest Commission on Colleges and Universities. It offers bachelor's and master's degrees in teaching, business, health professions, and information technologies. In addition to its use of "competency-based curricula" instead of contact hours, WGU's approach to curriculum development instruction differs from traditional institutions in that it outsources curriculum development, and faculty serve in the role of mentors and coaches to students who work through self-paced learning modules.

In June 2011, WGU reported an enrollment of twenty-five thousand and eleven thousand graduates. According to its annual report, "WGU is self-sustaining on tuition of $5,800 per 12-month year for most programs" and has only increased tuition $200 over a six-year period.[17] Despite some criticism from traditional colleges and universities regarding its unconventional approach to curriculum and instruction, the college has attracted investments from foundations such as Lumina and the Bill & Melinda Gates Foundation, and it has achieved promising results in just over a decade of operation. The college scored on par or above average on the National Survey of Student Engagement in the categories of overall educational experience, academic challenge, supportive campus environment, and academic advising. According to employer survey data, 98 percent of responding employers agreed that WGU graduates meet or exceed their expectations, 100 percent would not hesitate to hire another WGU graduate, 98 percent rate WGU graduates as equal to or better than graduates of other universities, and 98 percent consider WGU graduates strongly prepared for their jobs.[18]

Strategic Innovations at the Course Level

Unless they launch offshoots of their existing institutions, most community colleges do not have the luxury of starting from the ground up. Yet community colleges could adopt many of the strategies and approaches being used by New Community College, the Tennessee Technology Centers, and Western Governors University. Some colleges are beginning to advance transformative change and achieve breakthrough performance through course redesign initiatives. Among the first to identify and advance the use of technology for mass course redesign is the National Center for Academic Transformation (NCAT) under the direction of Carol Twigg. NCAT created a course redesign methodology designed to improve the quality of student learning while simultaneously increasing retention and reducing costs. Initially supported by the Pew Charitable Trusts and in partnership with thirty colleges, NCAT course-redesign projects focused on heavily enrolled, introductory courses that reach significant student numbers. Thus, even though the change focus is at the course level rather than an entire program, the NCAT design has the potential to affect institutionwide performance, considering that just twenty-five courses generate about 50 percent of student enrollment. "To have a significant impact on large numbers of students, an institution should concentrate on redesigning the 25 courses in which most students are enrolled instead of putting a lot of energy into technology investments in disparate small-enrollment courses."[19]

Course redesign is structured to address a fundamental challenge facing colleges. As new technologies capable of enhancing student learning and student outcomes continue to emerge, the tendency among colleges and universities is simply to adopt the new technologies and integrate them into existing courses without changing the systems, structure, or staffing mode. This strategy leads to growth in expense and inhibits the optimal use of the technology to maximize "time on task" for students and to reduce instructor time on repetitive and administrative tasks.

NCAT promotes five principles of course redesign for colleges and universities interested in participating:

Principle 1: Redesign the whole course.

Principle 2: Encourage active learning.

Principle 3: Provide students with individualized assistance.

Principle 4: Build in ongoing assessment and prompt (automated) feedback.

Principle 5: Ensure sufficient time on task and monitor student progress.[20]

The goal of redesigning the whole course is to achieve improved quality and reduced costs. By focusing on high-enrollment courses and requiring that the changes be made at the level of the course, rather than at the individual section level, colleges that engage in course redesign have the opportunity to overcome barriers that institutions encounter when scaling up pilot innovations. NCAT explains the rationale for redesigning the whole course as follows:

> The course is treated as a set of products and services that can be continuously worked on and improved by all faculty rather than as a "one-off" that gets re-invented by individual faculty members each term. The collective commitment of all faculty teaching the course coupled with the capabilities provided by information technology leads to success . . . Faculty can systematically incorporate feedback from all involved in the teaching and learning process, adding to, replacing, correcting and improving an ever-growing body of learning materials and best practices.[21]

According to NCAT, the collaboration among faculty who teach a single course helps prevent "course drift" and improves course coherence and the consistency of learning experiences for students. It also eliminates duplication of effort on the part of instructors and creates opportunities for alternative staffing patterns and cost savings. As NCAT explains,

> Faculty begin the design process by analyzing the amount of time that each person involved in the course spends on each kind of activity, which often reveals duplication of effort among multiple faculty members. Faculty members teaching the course divide their tasks among themselves and target their efforts to particular aspects of course delivery. By replacing individual development of each course section with shared responsibility for both course development and course delivery, faculty can save substantial amounts of their time while achieving greater course consistency.[22]

Course redesign also opens up possibilities for alternative staffing patterns in large introductory courses. Technology is used to replace some of the repetitive work required of faculty teaching traditional courses, thereby reducing the amount of time it takes faculty to serve a single student without detracting from the actual learning experience. This approach to redesign enables institutions to increase the number of students served without increasing faculty workload, while simultaneously improving student outcomes. It challenges the assumption held by many colleges and universities that lower faculty-to-student ratios improves the student learning experience. Course redesign methods promoted by NCAT open up the possibility that faculty can reduce the quantity of time spent and simultaneously improve the quality of the instructional experience for students.

Tallahassee Community College (TCC) in Florida initially became engaged in course redesign in 2001 after being awarded a Pew grant in conjunction with the National Center for Academic Transformation. Sally Search, dean of Academic Support at TCC, indicates that TCC's redesign of Freshman Composition "brought consistency to the course in terms of outcomes, assessment, and major writing assignments . . . [and] student success rates increased from less than 60 percent in Fall 2001 to 74 percent in Fall, 2010."[23] The work did not stop there. In 2007, TCC began a holistic redesign of developmental studies. As Search explains:

> The entire program was redesigned and aligned both vertically and horizontally allowing for greater consistency and cohesion within the program and individual disciplines. Like the redesign of Freshman Composition, this redesign also leverages technology to support individualized learning paths, focuses on active engagement with content, and promotes collaboration among students and faculty. Additionally, the developmental studies redesign integrates strategies to help students develop effective learning strategies and personal responsibility. The redesign was implemented in Fall 2009 and students who complete developmental studies are now outperforming those who placed directly into college-level English and mathematics.[24]

So why is redesign a value-added process? Some benefits are obvious: greater access for students, higher quality of instruction, effective and appropriate use of technology, greater consistency within courses, common learning outcomes and assessments, active learning, increased time on task, and improved retention resulting in decreased cost to the institution. Beyond that, the benefit to the faculty cannot be overlooked. The redesign process reenergizes faculty. It promotes professional development, recognizes talents and expertise, fosters innovation, promotes collegiality, provides opportunities for interdisciplinary dialog, and allows for the emergence of new leadership.

From Online and Blended Courses to Open Courseware

The National Center for Academic Transformation is one of a growing number of organizations working to deploy technology in innovative ways to transform learning and to improve student outcomes. Matthew Prineas and Marie Cini argue in a recent National Institute for Learning Outcomes Assessment (NILOA) Occasional Paper that new technology is just beginning to be used in ways that bring together the power of online learning and student outcomes assessment to improve teaching and learning.[25] They note that asynchronous master learning—a process whereby students demonstrate mastery at one level before progressing to the next—is becoming the dominant model for online learning. Technology is transforming the capability of institutions to perform learning outcomes assessment, which in turn has the potential to transform teaching and learning.

Whereas standard practice in assessment of learning outcomes in face-to-face classes is to assess only a small sample of students, new technology in online learning is making it possible for instructors to assess every student's progress toward mastering established learning outcomes in real time without requiring manual data collection and compilation.[26] They explain,

> Technology is also making possible the ability to track, assess, and respond to the behaviors and mastery levels of students in online courses with far greater depth and rapidity than ever before. These approaches enable faculty and course designers to make rapid changes in instructional practices and curriculum, and they empower students to make informed decisions.[27]

Technology in educational delivery systems such as Carnegie Mellon's Open Learning Initiative and the Khan Academy employ "computer-mediated approaches to mastery learning," making it possible for students with diverse backgrounds and prior learning experience to "begin with differing sets of baseline knowledge, progress at different rates, and master the course curriculum within different time frames."[28]

Carnegie Mellon's Open Learning Initiative (OLI) was initially conceived in 2001 to turn "cognitive tutoring" into online courses.[29] In 2002 four online courses (Causal and Statistical Reasoning, Statistics, Logic, and Economics) were developed with support from the William and Flora Hewlett Foundation. In 2010, Carnegie Mellon reached out to community colleges across the nation to adapt the course to their curriculum. As a result of feedback from community colleges, they increased the number of course applications by 33 percent and enhanced "practice activities in sections of the course where community college students typically struggle." Major sections of the course were restructured as "topics covered by community college curricula are often different from those included in the OLI Statistics course" and "support was added for statistical software tools and technologies commonly used at community colleges."[30]

The multi-institutional Cognitive Coursewares Design is an open course redesign initiative organized by the Association of Public Land Grant Colleges, the American Association of Community Colleges, and the Open Learning Initiative of Carnegie Mellon University.[31] Launched in 2011, the pilot experience will be implemented in 2012 to 2013. The initiative brings together two-year and four-year college and university faculty teams, assessment and instructional design experts, and other professionals to develop collaboratively six introductory courses: Precalculus, Psychology, Biology/ Life Science Majors, Biology/Life Science Nonmajors, Macroeconomics, and English Composition. The teams will reach consensus on learning outcomes, and courses and materials will be developed collaboratively to include web-based learning experiences, interactive technologies such as intelligent tutoring systems, virtual labs, simulations, and frequent opportunities for assessment and feedback. Once developed, the courseware will be made open access for individual students and available for institutional use as well. A modest fee structure will be used to defray costs. The project has the potential to create a framework for establishing a multi-institutional platform for high-demand gateway courses and to reduce the cost of providing core courses.

A leader in the open courseware movement, Massachusetts Institute of Technology now offers access to lectures, online textbooks, and tests for 2,100 MIT courses—nearly all undergraduate and graduate-level courses offered by the university—free of charge. According to MIT, each course published and made available online requires an investment of approximately $10,000 to $15,000.[32] The program does not allow students to earn a degree or credential, nor does it permit access to faculty or individual assistance with the material. The site simply makes the content of courses available as well as tools to help students learn course material. Self-directed learners move through the materials at their own pace. This program underscores the degree to which the "value" that colleges and universities deliver and what students pay for is not course content, but the experience that instructors provide in helping students learn and the credential students earn. Earning an MIT credential holds enough value in the marketplace that the university sees no risk in trying to protect the content a course delivers. MIT's open courseware represents an "unbundling" of knowledge creation, knowledge dissemination, and career preparation that is the traditional value proposition of postsecondary education.

As course content becomes more widely available online, its financial value declines. A core component of the value proposition of traditional colleges and universities rests on both the active teaching function and the credentialing function. MIT recently launched a new program, MITx, which allows students to earn certificates awarded by MITx. The platform includes interactive instruction, student-to-student, and student-to-professor communication, which enables students to demonstrate mastery and earn certificates. Launched in March 2012, students registering in the pilot were able to do so free of charge. In the future, MITx plans to charge a modest fee for participation.[33]

A nonprofit education provider, the Khan Academy markets itself as "a free world-class education for anyone anywhere."[34] Like OLI, the Khan Academy offers course modules free of charge to students. However, Khan Academy is a nonprofit organization providing learning modules that cover K–12 math, science, finance, and history. Anyone can access the materials, whether or not they are officially enrolled as a secondary school student anywhere in the world. The Khan Academy uses powerful analytics that enable students and teachers to chart individual progress. Software tracks where users are spending their time, what they have completed, and the knowledge, skills, and competencies they have mastered, as well as recommendations for where to go next. Performance data and recommendations are presented as a "knowledge map" to help users understand how knowledge, competencies, and skills fit together and build upon one another. This information also helps teachers track the progress of each of their students, as well as classroom-level data to get a snapshot of where the class is in its progress and level of mastery. As an incentive, students receive badges to denote specific levels of mastery.

New providers are beginning to enter the open courseware market, and for-profit providers are beginning to offer targeted services, such as tutoring, although they face greater barriers to entry than traditional colleges and universities. Smarthinking, a for-profit online tutoring company launched in 1999, provides on-demand tutoring in introductory courses for colleges seeking a more cost-effective way to provide tutoring or to supplement face-to-face tutoring services.[35] In 2008, StraighterLine, a spin-off of Smarthinking, began offering introductory, self-paced online college courses for a membership fee of $99 per month, rather than on a course-by-course basis. However, StraighterLine has encountered a major barrier since its initial launch. Unaccredited, it relies on partnerships with accredited four-year colleges and universities to accept the courses, and it has encountered resistance from potential partner institutions, as alumni and faculty question the quality of the courses and resist transfer and articulation agreements that would enable students to earn credits for StraighterLine courses from an accredited college or university.

Critics of StraighterLine have questioned the quality of the product it delivers. Given the interest of both critics and proponents of new entrants like StraighterLine, in 2010 Serena Golden of Inside Higher Education enrolled in an introductory macroeconomics course through StraighterLine and reported on the experience. Citing significant content and quality-control issues including lesson presentations unrelated to material in the textbooks, sloppiness in structure and content of the lesson materials, grammatical and typographical errors, and technological glitches, she raised questions about the quality of the experience.[36] As with newcomers in any industry, quality control challenges demonstrate a performance gap between "customer" expectations and the capacity of a new entrant to deliver a quality learning experience. The need to certify the quality of a product, through transfer agreements and/or accreditation, remains a barrier to upstarts like Straighter-Line, but not an insurmountable one. The models being developed today may be co-opted by accredited colleges and universities tomorrow as alternatives to traditional business models.

OFFERING NEW VALUE

As delivery platforms and business models change, colleges and universities will remain dependent upon partnerships to enhance and protect the value they provide. Partnerships are not new to community colleges. Partnerships with four-year colleges and universities are essential for community colleges to fulfill their transfer mission, and partnerships with employers are essential for community colleges to provide students with solid pathways to industries and occupations in demand.

Online platforms are enabling community colleges to take partnerships to new levels. As in the partnership launched between Carnegie Mellon University faculty and community college faculty working on online courses, or the partnerships developed between Stanford University faculty and community college faculty through the Carnegie Foundation for the Advancement of Teaching's Statway and Quantway projects, instructors are able to collaborate in course development and share expertise and results across institutions. Furthermore, students can be enrolled dually in courses at multiple institutions and earn bachelor's and master's degrees from partner institutions without leaving a community college campus. Lorain County Community College in Ohio, for example, enables students to earn bachelors' and masters' degrees from eight Ohio universities without leaving its campus. It is also one of the first community colleges to launch a community fabrication lab—"Fab Lab"—in partnership with MIT, and it is the first college in Ohio to offer podcast lectures on iTunesU. [37]

Online and computer-mediated learning opens up new possibilities for credentialing as well as possibilities for documenting knowledge and skills that may eventually rival certificates and degrees as proxies for learning. To date, one-year certificates, two-year degrees, and four-year degrees awarded by accredited colleges and universities have held their market value. However, as mastery learning becomes more heavily relied upon for documenting and tracking knowledge, accreditation rules may shift, or the accreditation process itself may lose value among employers, and ultimately, prospective students. In this scenario, the basis of value for community colleges will shift to the regional networks in which they serve as a nexus for students, employers, and content providers. Community colleges with strong networks that begin adopting alternative credentialing approaches could become a hub for satisfying unmet community needs. They could also play an important role in supplementing learning for traditional students and for paving the way for change in the way students engage in postsecondary education, demonstrate competencies and define completion.

From Possibility to Reality

These are but a few areas in which community colleges can use change strategies to create, not react to, a future that will be very different. The door is open to speculation on what lies ahead for our colleges. Now is the time to turn imagination loose and envision different possibilities for the future—our task in the Epilogue. A linear approach to thinking will not be enough to get the job done, at least not for colleges with ambitious goals and creative leaders. The future will belong to colleges that embrace change and leverage resources in pursuit of change. These colleges are not for everyone. They are for people who are able to see possibilities and find ways to turn possibilities into reality.

NOTES

1. Jamie Merisotis (president and CEO, Lumina Foundation), excerpted from an untitled essay submitted to the authors July 29, 2011.
2. Vijay Govindarajan and Chris Trimble, *Ten Rules for Strategic Innovators: From Idea to Execution* (Boston: Harvard Business Review Press, 2005), xxi.
3. Govindarajan and Trimble, *Ten Rules for Strategic Innovators*, xxiv.
4. Govindarajan and Trimble, *Ten Rules for Strategic Innovators*, xvii.
5. Lumina Foundation for Education, *A Stronger Nation through Higher Education*, September 2010, 3, http://www.luminafoundation.org/states_landing/a_stronger_nation_through_education/.
6. Stan Jones, "Freedom to Fail? The Board's Role in Reducing College Dropout Rates," *Trusteeship*, Association for Governing Boards, January–February 2011, 2.
7. Jones, "Freedom to Fail?" 2.
8. Stan Jones (president, Complete College America), excerpted from an untitled essay submitted to the authors July 29, 2011.
9. City University of New York, "A New Community College Concept Paper," August 18, 2011, and CUNY website, "About the New Community College Initiative," http://www1.cuny.edu/portal_ur/cmo/i/8/24/nccconceptpaper.pdf.
10. City University of New York website, "A New Community College Concept Paper."
11. City University of New York website, "A New Community College Concept Paper."
12. Scott Evenbeck (founding president, New Community College), excerpted from an essay, "The New Community College of the City University of New York," submitted to the authors July 25, 2012.
13. Evenbeck, "The New Community College of the City University of New York."
14. John Hoops, "A Working Model for Student Success: Tennessee Technology Centers—A Preliminary Case Study," Complete College America, June 2010, 11, http://www.completecollege.org/docs/Tennessee%20Technology%20Centers-%20A%20Preliminary%20Case%20Study(1).pdf.

15. Jeff Selingo, "A Disrupted Higher-Ed System, Next (blog), The Chronicle of Higher Education, January 26, 2012, http://chronicle.com/blogs/next/2012/01/26/a-disrupted-higher-ed-system/.

16. Western Governor's University, "The WGU Story," http://www.wgu.edu/about_WGU/WGU_story (accessed May 28, 2012).

17. Western Governor's University, Annual Report 2011, http://www.wgu.edu/about_WGU/annual_report_2011.pdf, 3.

18. Western Governor's University, Annual Report 2011, 5.

19. Carol Twigg, "Course Redesign Improves Learning and Reduces Cost," *Policy Alert*, National Center for Public Policy and Higher Education, June 2005, 2.

20. National Center for Academic Transformation, "Five Principles of Successful Course Redesign," http://www.thencat.org/R2R/R2R%20PDFs/SuccCrsRed.pdf.

21. National Center for Academic Transformation, "Five Principles of Successful Course Redesign."

22. National Center for Academic Transformation, "Five Principles of Successful Course Redesign."

23. Sally Search (dean, Academic Support Division, Tallahassee Community College), excerpted from an essay "Course Redesign: A Value-Added Process," submitted to the authors June 28, 2011.

24. Search, "Course Redesign: A Value-Added Process."

25. Matthew Prineas and Marie Cini, "Assessing Learning in Online Education: The Role of Technology in Improving Student Outcomes" (Occasional Paper @12, National Institute for Learning Outcomes Assessment, Champaign, Illinois, October 2011), 4, http://www.learningoutcomeassessment.org/documents/onlineed.pdf.

26. Prineas and Cini, "Assessing Learning in Online Education," 4.

27. Prineas and Cini, "Assessing Learning in Online Education," 6.

28. Prineas and Cini, "Assessing Learning in Online Education," 9.

29. Carnegie Mellon University, "Open Learning Initiative: Learn More about OLI," http://oli.cmu.edu/get-to-know-oli/learn-more-about-oli/ (accessed June 8, 2012).

30. Carnegie Mellon University, "The Herb Simon Connection," http://oli.cmu.edu/the-herb-simon-connection/ (accessed June 8, 2011).

31. "Multi-institutional Cognitive Coursewares Design Solicitation for Participation, http://www.aplu.org/page.aspx?pid=2090 (accessed May 28, 2012).

32. Massachusetts Institute of Technology, MIT Open Courseware, http://ocw.mit.edu/about/.

33. MIT's News Office, "MITx: MIT's New Online Learning Initiative," December 19, 2011, http://mitx.mit.edu/6002x-press-release.html.

34. Khan Academy, "About the Khan Academy," http://www.khanacademy.org/about (accessed May 28, 2012).

35. Kevin Carey, "College for $99 a Month," *Washington Monthly*, September/October 2009, http://www.washingtonmonthly.com/college_guide/feature/college_for_99_a_month.php.

36. Serena Golden, "A Curricular Innovation, Examined," InsideHigherEd.com, December 16, 2010, http://www.insidehighered.com/news/2010/12/16/review_of_straighterline_online_courses.

37. Lorain County Community College FabLab, http://www.lorainccc.edu/academic+divisions/engineering+technologies/fab+lab (accessed June 9, 2012).

Epilogue: Perspective and a Change in Focus

Brick and mortar campuses may become a thing of the past. It is more likely, however, that they will become the premium, the luxury option for higher education.[1]
—Scott Bowman, Central Queensland University, Australia

In this book we have provided an overview of the societal fabric in which community colleges emerged, the characteristics that came to define them as they grew and flourished throughout the twentieth century, the paradox embedded in these characteristics, and challenges they face in the years ahead. Chapter 1 described the growth and development of community colleges. Chapter 2 disclosed the challenges leaders face in managing paradox and building a capacity for change and innovation. Chapter 3 examined continuous improvement efforts and innovations underway to improve learning outcomes. And chapter 4 explored what might be considered disruptive innovations that community colleges are beginning to implement to meet the growing demand for advanced knowledge and skills in a global economy.

In the Epilogue we come full circle and explore the changing landscape of higher education and the unfinished revolution of community colleges within this landscape. We begin with a question: Are community colleges on the threshold of restructuring? From there we examine different scenarios for the future in the form of trends and possibilities as community colleges seek to fulfill their core purpose. Their success in doing so is paramount. Not only are learners from diverse backgrounds looking to community colleges for goal fulfillment, the nation itself is looking to them for leveraging its competitive position in a global economy.

A RESTRUCTURED INDUSTRY?

Are community colleges an industry on the threshold of restructuring? The answer could be "yes" or "no" depending on the perspective taken on restructuring. Two perspectives are described below, each leading to the same result: a loss of organizational equilibrium as environmental forces and competitors working with new business models coalesce to disrupt industry structure.

Restructuring and Organizational Performance

Restructuring can be induced by a shift in the relationship between key drivers that determine how an organization functions. In the case of colleges and universities, it is a shift in the relationship between demand, resources, capacity, and accountability. Historically, these drivers have operated in direct relationship to one another, with rising demand accompanied by a growth in resources and capacity while accountability remained constant. Community colleges have enjoyed an advantage over traditional institutions in a growth industry because of their unduplicated role in providing access to learners. They evolved to meet market demand for postsecondary education and training that four-year colleges and universities would not or could not accommodate. Their business model was simple: grow by keeping entry and operating costs low, acquire and deploy resources to support growth, and don't wait for rivals to catch up. This model put our colleges on the map, and leaders embraced and acted on it with unbridled enthusiasm.

Now, however, demand operates in an inverse relationship to resources and accountability. In the *new normal*, community colleges are expected to do more and better with less. Global competition has placed mounting pressure on companies to attract and retain a highly skilled workforce and on community colleges to prepare more and better workers. Never has the demand been higher for programs that build industry-prime knowledge and skills in a convenient and cost-effective manner. Yet the broad brushstroke of public opinion research and media headlines points to a growing perception that colleges and universities are either oblivious to emerging trends or have simply been incapable of implementing the changes necessary to address them. Consequently, it is increasingly common to hear industry insiders refer to the American system of higher education as a "broken business model." A burgeoning sense of dissatisfaction combined with eroding funding streams, growing resistance to tuition increases, and fast-moving competitors point to an industry poised for restructuring.

This shift in the relationship among demand, resources, and accountability has affected every aspect of how community colleges operate, including how they interpret their mission, how they distribute enrollment, how they deliver programs and services, and how they hire and deploy staff. It has also altered the relationship among stakeholders, including college leaders, boards, students, faculty and staff, payers (funding agencies), policymakers, and beneficiaries (employers). As demand and accountability expectations grow and resources diminish, a widening of the gap between "expected" and "actual" performance occurs where outputs lag behind stakeholder expectations. A "crisis of credibility" develops, and institutions become the target of criticism for failing to deliver desired results. Fairly or unfairly, they are labeled as "underachievers"—a circumstance that leads to the expansion of accountability mandates from payers and regulatory agencies, the vulnerability to market competition from rivals, and the increased bargaining power of customers (students) and beneficiaries (employers). A residual effect of underachiever status is added resource strain for institutions already under pressure to do more and better with less.

Restructuring and Disruptive Change

Restructuring can also be induced by shifting "consumer" needs and disruptive change as new entrants transform an industry by delivering a product or service that is better or costs less than existing providers.[2] This process has occurred in the steel industry, the information technology services industry, and the news media industry, among others.[3]

Projections of what a "disrupted" higher education industry might look like are now being advanced by industry experts and practitioners. Four ingredients come together to trigger industry disruption: technological enablers, value network adjustments, a shift in standards and the regulatory environment, and innovations to the business model (that is, the value proposition; processes and resources to deliver the value proposition; the profit formula; and competitive strategy).[4] The "competitive structure of the industry"[5] shifts as new business models create and deliver "greater value for customers."[6] For example, although colleges and universities have integrated new technology into existing business models, a failure to adjust to innovative business practices used by fast-moving competitors could leave traditional providers, including community colleges, unable to provide equivalent value, thereby making them vulnerable to enrollment and resource downturns.

On the whole, the value proposition that community colleges offer—access, low cost, convenience, and market relevant programs—has increased in relevance. However, educational institutions do more than simply deliver a product or service—they deliver learning experiences designed to enable students to earn a meaningful credential. Learning is not a static commodity. The learning experiences that students need and expect in a global landscape are changing—an indication that a corresponding shift in the value proposition is warranted, particularly in the way that it is achieved.

Addressing shifting conditions and needs requires innovation. Community colleges have repeatedly demonstrated their capacity for change and innovation, yet a question remains. Given organizational constraints, shifting environmental forces, and a dominant business model, can community colleges deliver on their current value proposition, let alone provide enhanced value, to meet the needs of their constituents? Addressing these challenges will require innovation beyond incremental improvement; however, success in implementing breakthrough innovations requires that community colleges adopt a business model that is suitable for innovation.

Community colleges currently operate with a business model and value network dominant among traditional higher education providers:

- They excel in the delivery of core value propositions (knowledge proliferation and learning, and preparation for life and a career)[7] and business functions (value-adding process businesses and facilitated user networks) central to traditional colleges and universities.[8]
- They address core value propositions by providing learning experiences that are packaged into credit-based courses organized around learning outcomes and activities developed by a single faculty member and delivered face-to-face, online, or hybrid over a specified number of "contact hours" that, when combined with courses in a given content area, lead to a degree or certificate.
- They use a multidimensional business model that "leverages interdependencies between employers and students" as well as students and four-year universities in delivering learning and credentialing.[9]

To the extent that community colleges are built around two core business propositions—knowledge proliferation and learning and preparation for life and a career—altering their business model is a less complex endeavor than altering the business model used by a research university. Alternative business models include unbundled models, whereby core business functions requiring different types of expertise—customer relationship management, product innovation, and infrastructure management—are separated, with some being performed by the organization, some by partners, and some outsourced completely. Another model is the facilitated network, whereby an organization empowers "customers to access and use a mix of products and services offered by multiple organizations," similar to patient-centered networks in the health care industry.[10]

As previous chapters have indicated, however, community colleges face numerous challenges in delivering core functions, and their effectiveness in doing so has been called into question. As alternative providers of both learning opportunities and credentialing emerge, community colleges will need to be innovative in the delivery of core functions by adopting business models capable of encouraging and supporting innovation. In short, community colleges will need to finish the revolution initiated when they emerged on the higher education scene over one hundred years ago.

BEYOND RESTRUCTURING

Perspective is often enhanced by distance, as the Impressionist painters knew very well. Looking outside the United States and the Western world to a system of higher education that has been described as currently enjoying a "golden age" (based upon political favor, funding, and innovation) provides a perspective on what the future may hold for American higher education, including community colleges.

Australia's economy has been among only a few in the world that has actually grown, even thrived, during the early twenty-first-century global economic downturn. Australia's prime minister, Julia Gillard, lifted existing funding caps and generously invested both in research and in the overall expansion of higher education. Adopting a regional approach, she charged each geographic region of Australia to develop its own future plan for higher education, and she appointed an overseer in each region to ensure that these plans had as a priority higher levels of participation (enrollment) and the completion of employer-recognized credentials. Nearly $2 billion in funding was set aside for the Australian Commonwealth to negotiate linkages between federally funded universities and the Vocational Education Training (VET) system, Australia's closest equivalent to community colleges. It is important to note that the VET includes both state-funded Tertiary and Further Education (TAFE) providers and private providers of job training. The outcome: new business models, seamless pathways, increased innovation and competition—all to develop a more educated citizenry and the skilled workforce required to sustain the nation's robust economy.

THE UNFINISHED REVOLUTION

Remedying Weaknesses, Vulnerabilities, and Shortfalls

It is no secret that community colleges have low degree completion rates. It is also no secret that given the nation's increasing reliance on them for advanced education and workforce development, there is an urgent need to get to the root of the problem. Is the problem caused by deficiencies in community colleges, deficiencies in students attending community colleges, or both? The answer is obviously "both," but the way in which community colleges organize and deliver instruction and support services is a contributing factor. Community colleges have evolved rapidly with little clear design. This is especially obvious in organizational procedures that guide or fail to guide students through college—particularly underlying assumptions that guide institutional actions.[11] According to James Rosenbaum, Julie Redline, and Jennifer Stephan in "Community College: The Unfinished Revolution," community colleges assume that students have the know-how to direct their own progress—an assumption that is often faulty. Many students do not have a plan or work with vague and unrealistic plans. Colleges also assume that students are capable of making informed choices from a bewildering maze of programs, curricula, courses, and delivery options. Finally, colleges assume that students possess the social skills and job-search skills to locate and successfully obtain appropriate jobs—many do not.[12]

Rosenbaum, Redline, and Stephan further the analysis of misassumptions by describing the effect of "information overload" on student success.[13] Community colleges allow students to explore broadly in liberal arts and to progress at their own pace, assuming that they have clear plans and can assess which classes will fulfill those plans. When students have information or logistical problems, community colleges respond by making more information available in electronic or print form—brochures, catalogue pages, course descriptions, policy statements, and more. For students unfamiliar with college and inexperienced with handling large amounts of information, information overload can result. In providing more options, community colleges also create complex pathways that confuse students and deter them from goal achievement.[14] Options also overwhelm institutions; colleges have difficulty offering required courses in the semesters when students need them and during time slots that fit students' schedules. In contrast, if a specific set of courses were stipulated for degree completion, course offerings were reduced, and courses were scheduled in predetermined time slots so that schedules remained constant throughout the year, a college would be able to offer the necessary courses in the right term, and students could make steady progress.[15]

Finally, "reward obscurity" acts as a deterrent to student progress and goal achievement. Community colleges assume that students have the motivation to persevere through the many challenges—financial, academic, and personal—that stand in the way of earning a college degree. However, motivation requires the ability to envision and maintain progress toward eventual rewards, and community colleges may inadvertently make it difficult for students to make discernible progress toward rewards.[16] For instance, community colleges have extended the course schedule well beyond the standard Monday through Friday nine-to-five schedule. Students can take classes in the early mornings, evenings, and weekends—a well-intentioned move that provides flexibility but just as readily can create complexity and time conflicts that students cannot manage.[17] Students have difficulty coordinating work and childcare with complex class schedules that may change every semester. They cannot anticipate when courses will be offered in future semesters or whether they can be coordinated with other responsibilities. This uncertainty can diminish student confidence in completing a degree because too many barriers stand in the way of steady progress.[18]

In considering these impediments to student success in tandem with the changing postsecondary education landscape and the handful of community colleges that have successfully altered the dominant business model, it is reasonable to conclude that while the recommendations set forth in the report of the 21st Century Commission on the Future of Community Colleges ("Reclaiming the American Dream") may help to establish a direction for the future, they do not—and should not be expected to—present a guidebook for future success. What is certain is that there is no guidebook. In one sense, the Commission's recommendations for redesigning the educational experience of learners, reinventing institutional roles, and resetting the system aptly capture key elements of the current challenge. In another sense, however, the Commission's recommendations must be seen as remedial—catch-up steps for an enterprise that is producing outputs that fall short of stakeholder expectations.

Efforts to redesign the educational experience of students, one of the Commission's recommendations, are actively underway at community colleges throughout the nation. Many of these efforts are being incentivized by leading foundations (e.g., the Carnegie Foundation's support of community college participation in the Quantway project and the National Center for Academic Transformation's support of course redesign projects). It is likely that growing public awareness of low completion rates, skills gaps (companies are unable to locate and hire high-skilled workers), and the developmental problem will induce institutions to work with urgency and dispatch in building new models for the educational experience. Whether or not one or more of these new models will qualify as disruptive innovation has yet to be seen. Educational service providers like Blackboard and K–12, Incorporated, have combined their know-how and resources to produce comprehensive, online developmental courses taught by developmental and subject-area specialists. Similar products and services are under development, but until the overarching question of who owns precollege basic skills—K–12 or higher education—and how to finance precollegiate coursework are answered, lasting solutions are unlikely to be forthcoming.

Acknowledging that "a reimagined community college cannot yet be fully defined," the 21st Century Commission recommended a framework for change involving a change in focus:

- from expanding access to access and improvement in student success and completion;
- from fragmented curricular construction (course accruals) to clear and coherent educational pathways;
- from tolerance of underpreparedness to the elimination of achievement gaps;
- from a culture of anecdote-based to a culture of evidence-based decision making;
- from individual to collective responsibility for student success;
- from a culture of isolation to a culture of collaboration;
- from a cottage-industry approach to education at scale;
- from primacy of teaching to primacy of learning;
- from infomatics to learning analytics; and
- from enrollment-based funding to enrollment/institutional performance/ student success-based funding.

It is possible that the change in perspective and focus recommended by the Commission will be embraced by institutions and leaders and will guide fundamental change at community colleges. However, in the absence of major investment and incentives to create new funding models, new staffing models, and new content and delivery models, the creation and implementation of new structures and systems will continue to be spotty and unscalable.

The Unfinished Revolution: Partnerships, Acquisitions, Alliances, and Networks

Partnerships are ingrained in the history and present-day structure of community colleges. In the future, financial constraints and the growing demand for access to higher education—particularly the industry demand for stackable credentials that allow for the development of core knowledge and skills and industry-specific occupational skills—will intensify pressure on community colleges to develop and use partnerships to achieve their core mission. In addition, the sheer number of postsecondary institutions in today's market, and the growing number of students who swirl among institutions in order to earn their degrees, will also intensify this pressure.

The need for economy, specialization, and scale are primary drivers that motivate the formation of new partnerships.[19] Successful partnerships allow players to leverage the unique attributes and advantages of one another. In an EDUCAUSE article, Daniel Pianko and Josh Jarrett highlight the growing prevalence of nonprofit/for-profit academic partnerships, explaining that nonprofits offer advantages of "lower costs of student acquisition, established brands, and deep faculty/academic expertise," whereas for-profits offer the advantage of "business expertise, experience with non-traditional students, access to investment capital, and scale economies."[20] As just one example, they note that the annual investment in improvement in teaching and learning made by the University of Phoenix ($200 million, or 4 percent of its revenue) dwarfs investments most individual colleges can make and will eventually amount to a significant advantage in quality over traditional colleges and universities.[21]

As the number, range, and depth of partnerships between educational institutions, employers, nonprofits, and for-profit organizations grow, community colleges must ensure that they have the leadership and organizational infrastructure necessary to leverage partnerships. Community college leaders will need to cultivate and create partnership opportunities to advance the mission of their institutions and, equally important, they must establish the organizational infrastructure and capacity to define and manage partnerships.

In Central Queensland, Australia, a merger of all regional, publicly supported institutions of higher education is currently underway. Regional employers, particularly in the mining and gas industries, are calling for improvements in the well-established Tertiary and Further Education (TAFE) sector, including faster response time, modern equipment for training, and on-site training in remote regions. According to Scott Bowman, vice chancellor of Central Queensland University (CQU), which is responsible for managing the merger, "dialogue about collaboration through articulation culminated in a decision to adopt a dual sector or 'merger and acquisition' approach to collaboration.[22] Carefully considered arguments were presented by parties on both sides, but the dual-sector model tested earlier in Victoria has shown considerable promise as a model for the future of higher education in Australia." The merger is moving forward, with some progress having already been achieved relative to curriculum mapping (e.g., refrigeration to engineering, LPN to RN, etc.). Clear pathways have been under development for some time, but "pathways or inter-sector transfer really get down to the department level." In other words, agreements between a university department and a TAFE department, which means that the going is slow.

The CQU merger is being funded with a $72 million investment by Australia's federal government. All parties involved in the dual-sector merger seem to agree that managing the integration of cultures has been, and will continue to be, the most difficult challenge. For example, TAFE leaders in Central Queensland worry that universities will ultimately dominate and that the established TAFE role and mission, which is about preparing people for jobs, will be lost or become a lesser priority. They also worry that the higher-education pecking order will continue to prevail, with one telling exception—institutions that have been least responsive to new markets, new modes of delivery, and so forth. These institutions, particularly those who built their business models on "imports" and international markets, have been forced to change due to a 2012 federal funding adjustment that promotes public-private partnerships and ties funding to enrollment growth. Australia's new focus is on strengthening educational pathways that lead to gainful employment and promote the nation's economic advancement.

At the University of Southern Queensland (USQ), Australia's recognized leader in the delivery of distance education, articulation won out over a merger as a means of advancing national higher education goals. In 2011, TAFE, Queensland, and USQ signed an agreement to allow students working and learning anywhere in Queensland to access seamless pathways into a university degree. Regional TAFE institutes provide classroom and face-to-face support for students enrolled in USQ's online courses in a range of industries and careers. According to USQ retired vice chancellor Bill Lovegrove, "The initiative is in response to the Federal Government's recommendation to build Australia's skill base and promote regional sustainability, through the provision of personally, professionally, industrially and regionally relevant educational pathways."[23]

Significant efficiencies are expected by avoiding resource duplication. For example, by using existing TAFE facilities, students enrolled externally will have the added benefit of accessing a range of support services that normally would not be available because of their remoteness from USQ campuses. As Lovegrove explained:

> By combining USQ's online capabilities and expertise as well as TAFE Queensland's physical and vocational resources and its local knowledge of the vocational educational and training sector, we will be able to develop a 21st Century teaching model that utilises flexible and interactive platforms at their best, without the significant cost and restructuring involved in establishing a dual-sector institution.[24]

There is little doubt that on the basis of economics alone, America's community colleges are being—and will continue to be—reshaped by mergers, partnerships, and alliances across all sectors of education, business, and not-for-profit organizations. In the State University of New York, a bold experiment in "shared services" led Chancellor Nancy Zimpher to merge agricultural and technical colleges—Delhi, Cobleskill, Morrisville, and SUNY IT—under the leadership of a single president. According to Chancellor Zimpher:

> Financial constraints in recent years have resulted in less course availability on our campuses, causing students to spend more time and money to complete their degrees. Strategically aligning our campuses where appropriate, puts SUNY in a stronger position to reverse this trend. Shared leadership between these campuses will best serve current and future students by enabling campuses to enroll more students, hire more full-time faculty, and increase course offerings.[25]

Zimpher expected the shared-services model to serve as a vehicle for cost savings across the sixty-five community colleges, agricultural and technical colleges, comprehensive colleges, and universities that comprise the State University of New York system. However, in late 2012, the SUNY Board reversed Zimpher's decision, announcing that each SUNY campus will have a president going forward.

Another initiative underway at SUNY is a seamless transfer process designed to streamline the transfer of credits between two-year and four-year colleges. Recognizing that student enrollment patterns are changing and pressure for efficiency from legislators is growing, two-plus-two agreements are being expanded to include college and university programs on community college campuses. Programs of this type are certainly not novel for community colleges. Partnerships with four-year colleges and universities enabling students to continue study toward the baccalaureate degree without leaving the community college campus have been successfully implemented by Macomb Community College (Michigan), Lorain County Community College (Ohio), Onondaga Community College (New York), and a smattering of community colleges throughout the nation. [26]

A challenge facing multiorganization networks is the need to create road maps for students that enable them to smoothly move through the system to degree completion. Needed are educational/occupational "GPS" systems with well-marked destinations, alternate pathways that can be easily rerouted, and convenient on and off ramps. A 2012 announcement heralding the educational alliance between the University of Phoenix and Northern Virginia Community College (NOVA) is an outstanding example of networks that are being established to advance student completion. At the heart of this alliance is seamless transition to bachelor's degree programs in health care, information technology, and criminal justice at the University of Phoenix for NOVA associate-degree holders. University of Phoenix brings to the alliance resources and brand reputation, a Prior Learning Assessment (PLA) system to award college credit for prior training and work experience, optional delivery modes to accommodate student schedules and preferences, and discounted tuition. NOVA brings college-tested, baccalaureate-ready students to the alliance. The University of Phoenix–NOVA alliance is noteworthy because of its sheer size, not necessarily its caché as innovation.

The ability to clarify and articulate value added for students, employers, and partners—particularly with regard to "completion"—will differentiate community colleges that achieve success in regional networks. A Community College Research Center (CCRC) research brief summarizing practices of high-performance organizations prepared by Davis Jenkins of CCRC identified best practices for continuous improvement in community colleges ranging from setting learning outcomes and completion goals to evaluating and improving alignment efforts. When combined with leadership focused on outcomes and partnerships with high schools, four-year colleges, and employers, these practices work to enhance organizational learning and ultimately leverage performance.[27] Given limited literature on organizational effectiveness in higher education and a conspicuous absence of research on partnerships between community colleges and four-year institutions and employers, Jenkins points to private-sector studies that demonstrate that firms that strategically manage relationships with "supplier and customer firms" perform better than their counterparts.[28] This evidence suggests that as community colleges work to align organizational architecture in support of completion, they must also sharpen their focus on management of external partnerships, given their significant potential for innovation.

Multidirectional Pathways between Education and Work

> The United States is unable to help people match their educational preparation with their career ambitions—not because it cannot be done but because it simply is not being done. All the information required to align postsecondary educational choices with careers is available, but unused.[29]
> —Georgetown University Center on Education and the Workforce

Data published by the Bureau of Labor Statistics (BLS) indicate that demand for individuals with postsecondary credentials will continue to grow. In a report titled *Help Wanted*, researchers at the Georgetown University Center on Education and the Workforce project a deficit of three million college graduates by 2018.[30] In a 2011 report from the Center on Education and the Workforce, *What's It Worth? The Economic Value of College Majors*, researchers present analyses describing the "economic value" of specific college baccalaureate degree majors.[31] Their research identifies occupational fields in which employers will have the greatest demand for college graduates, as well as fields with the greatest economic benefit. These reports suggest that colleges and universities are not doing enough to align their programs with industry needs. Further, federal and state government agencies and employers must do a better job of integrating labor market data and college and university data to provide students with better information about jobs in demand as well as educational pathways that will prepare them for these jobs.

National survey results also demonstrate a growing perception among employers and families that colleges are not doing enough to design education and training programs that cultivate knowledge and skills needed at different career stages to succeed in the workforce. Further, programs do not take into account obstacles adult learners face in concurrently pursuing education and work. A 2009 national survey conducted by the Business Roundtable, *The Springboard Project American Workforce Survey*, found that a majority (81 percent) of working adults who completed the survey indicated a willingness to participate in training and education outside the workplace, yet factors of convenience, inflexibility, and cost were obstacles to participation.[32] The Roundtable advocated that colleges more directly address workforce development needs of employers and incumbent and emerging workers by increasing program convenience and flexibility, by seeking the involvement of employers to ensure alignment, and by developing nationally recognized certifications.[33] The Roundtable advocated that businesses take a more active role in initiating partnerships with colleges and universities, leading and supporting the use of nationally recognized industry certifications, rewarding employees for credential completion, making improvement of the U.S. education system "a key part of corporate citizenship agendas," and actively communicating workplace expectations.[34]

Recently released public opinion survey results reveal a significant increase in the extent to which students and families view college enrollment and completion as essential to career opportunity. For example, nearly 86 percent of students surveyed by UCLA in 2011 as part of the American Freshman Survey ranked "to be able to get a better job" as "very important," up from 70 percent in 2006.[35] This trend reflects growing anxiety about the labor market and signals a growing expectation among students that their home institution understands the connection between education and a career and assigns top priority to developing knowledge and skills in demand in the workforce and credentials that will help them obtain and succeed in a job with prospects for continued advancement. The fact that students list job preparation as their top priority does not diminish the important role that colleges and universities play in facilitating learning for the sake of learning, or for other ends, such as developing civic engagement and awareness and enhancing the quality of life.[36] It does demonstrate, however, that institutions must place career preparation closer to the center of their value proposition.

Comprehensive community colleges by definition include a focus on both transfer and career programs. The research available suggests that in the future, community colleges will need to do a better job—in part through strategic partnerships—of informing students at all career stages of the pathways available to them and the related education and training programs that will move them along those pathways. They will also need to advocate for better data at the state level through the establishment of a statewide database that tracks learners through secondary to postsecondary education and into the workforce, along the lines of the system developed and implemented in the state of Florida.[37]

Mass Customization, i-Learning, and Shifting Faculty Roles

If completion rates are to improve, a key challenge will be to tackle student success at the individual level, focusing on whole-person development and preparing learners who can think and act effectively in the information age. Instructors at community colleges with heavy teaching loads and more-often-than-not adjunct status play a primary role in meeting, or failing to meet, this challenge. Though alarmist in tone, there is veracity to a recent blog by Jonathan Alter indicating that "every faculty member at every institution must be engaged in the vital work of keeping students in school . . . otherwise, we're all going down together."[38] Further complicating already complex teaching and learning dynamics is the reality that student-consumers are going to be the primary driver in the future.

Technology promises to provide the tools and the capacity needed to respond to individual needs and demands in a more systematic and efficient manner. Even as community colleges shift to hybrid delivery models, the traditional stand-and-deliver instructional paradigm is firmly planted and will present a formidable barrier to meaningful change in the educational experience of students. Faculty sign on to teach discipline-specific content, which is in keeping with their educational preparation and career inclinations. They do not readily agree to act as learning coaches and facilitators or to use modern tools of technology to produce specific learning outcomes for students as part of an individualized approach to instruction. Still, it is likely those institutions that are best able to understand their client base, and respond accordingly, who will survive and prosper in the years ahead.

In her article in *Game Changers: Education and Information Technologies*, Diana Oblinger, president and CEO of EDUCAUSE, argues,

> Today, courses may be better thought of as tools to manage time, staff and resources or as building blocks for the discipline. However, the bounded, self-contained course can no longer be the central unit of analysis of the curriculum because it may no longer be the place where the most significant learning takes place.[39]

Oblinger highlights "features of valuable learning experiences, which may be found inside or outside of courses enabled by information technology," such as:

- "the professional-amateur ('pro-am') approach to learning," whereby more experienced learners support those who are less experienced;
- infusing "real-world problems that matter" to students, using technology through simulations, virtual environments, gaming, open-innovation networks, and other approaches;

- "feed-forward" systems that provide feedback and assistance in future decisions by "suggesting the next course or experience";
- using technology to provide students with "structured autonomy," whereby students receive structure and support for semi-self-directed learning, through supports such as motivation, a road map or pathway, and through "the prompts, guides, and hints that can help learners past obstacles," such as those offered through Carnegie Mellon University's Open Learning Initiative (OLI);
- enhanced student support services, such as portals, learning commons, integrated support, e-portfolios; and
- peer-to-peer programs, such as OpenStudy (http://www.openstudy.com) and Grockit (http://grockit.com/), which comprise an online social-studying network, with participants in 170 countries.[40]

In addition, technology can support career and academic program exploration through services such as Career Cruising (http://www.careercruising. com/us/en), and external service providers that deliver credentialing assistance such as Parchment (http://www.parchment.com), which "allow users to request, store, and send educational credentials . . . use transcripts to compare user credentials to what colleges require, and provide recommendations about where students should apply."[41]

According to Wide Bay vice chancellor and president Bill Lovegrove, new competition will drive contemporary, high-quality program development, and "stimulating and inspiring change for the education provider (faculty) will be the primary challenge of the future. Institutions that do not manage this well will be 'easy pickings' in the increasingly competitive industry of higher education." Sophisticated "customer service" systems are being supported by information technology (IT) today, but for instruction and support services, delivering the human touch is the most critical part of effective IT systems in higher education. Skype, for example, uses technology to expand human-to-human interaction, but the human element is lacking in most higher-education IT-based education and student support systems. Borderless education is the goal, blurring distinctions between face-to-face and online learning and support services, using technology to its fullest effect to deliver a personalized, high-touch educational experience. The challenge that community colleges face is to think from the learner's perspective and change as necessary to operate from that vantage point.

It is a certainty that technological advances will continue to enable advances in the content and delivery of instruction and related support services, probably in ways that cannot even be imagined today. The best new technologies will support ever-higher levels of personalized, customized educational experiences. And existing and new technologies will be used more effectively to give students the personal attention they want and need at the front door of the higher education experience. For example, students will have expanded opportunities to self-test and self-prepare (e.g., new online developmental education programming) to avoid spending time and money on basic skills development. Technology will deliver effective tools for translating experience into college credit, and for unbundling curricular requirements so as to help students move step-by-step from high school diploma to different levels of higher education and credentialing.

Today's traditional Carnegie-based design discourages many students who simply cannot see the light at the end of the tunnel and, thereby, add to the swell of attrition statistics. Technology will enable students to explore options, interests, and job opportunities in advance of enrolling in an academic program, again saving time and money. Technology and new approaches to instruction will make it possible for colleges and universities to switch from "seat time" and grades as indicators of progress to assessing learning while offering flexibility in the time required to complete a credential by increasing the use of self-paced learning and prior-learning assessments. These advances will require the development of a viable financial model for certification services, as well as a set of academic standards shared by multiple institutions. This shift will require considerable effort, but some institutions are taking initial steps to prepare for this transition. Examples include Western Governor's University, colleges and universities that have participated in the NCAT Course Redesign initiative, and open courseware initiatives. In addition, national organizations are working to develop frameworks that will support these efforts, including the Voluntary System of Accountability sponsored by the Association of Public and Land-grant Universities and the Association of State Colleges and Universities, the Voluntary Framework of Accountability developed by the American Association of Community Colleges and the College Board, and the draft Degree Qualifications Framework developed by the Lumina Foundation. [42]

A system for intrainstitutional and interinstitutional data sharing to support mass customization will become increasingly important in the future, but the likelihood of developing a user-friendly K–16 IT/data system seems particularly remote in light of the current state of relationships between K–12 school districts and colleges and universities. Australia has made some progress on this front, but significant challenges have arisen in the first phase of IT/data integration between area high schools and TAFE Ultimo in New South Wales. Curriculum mapping is in place across institutions, but the development of mutually agreeable content and faculty training have been obstacles to forward progress.

Continued progress toward the effective and innovative use of technology to enhance community college programs, services, and delivery will, no doubt, be the shape of the future. Minding the quality of programming, particularly online and distance delivery, will be as important as innovation.

Fueled by new funding models and increased demand, competition will be greater than ever. The future of competition, however, will be the leveraging of quality through leaders and institutions committed to innovation.

IN CLOSING

Were community colleges a disruptive innovation when they emerged on the higher education scene at the beginning of the twentieth century? Perhaps. The advent of the community college definitely made higher education available to significantly more people by virtue of affordability and proximity, but by and large, this innovation did not result in a new business model relative to funding, staffing, systems, and culture. Throughout their history, community colleges have been remarkably successful at adopting innovations initiated by other organizations. Take online delivery of programming and services, for example. Community colleges now dominate the online education market. It was the University of Phoenix, however, that put all of the pieces together to successfully launch this new business model and bring it to the higher education market twenty years ago, thereby disrupting the industry. Community colleges have also captured the lion's share of the dual enrollment, remedial education, and workforce education markets. These new markets were secured largely as a result of increased demand and competitive advantage (e.g., pricing), not as a result of innovation. As to their future role in advancing the kinds of innovation that might qualify as industry game changers, our research suggests that it is improbable that community colleges will lead the way in innovation. Innovations currently underway in community colleges tend to be incremental, sporadic, isolated, and more often than not, unscalable. In addition, they are seldom the result of carefully planned and executed research and development, nor are they the outcome of a culture that values and pursues innovation.

Not surprisingly, perpetually scarce resources and the accretion over time of inefficient systems and practices common to the higher education industry have coalesced to impede the ability of community colleges to establish structures and systems that are conducive to scalable and sustainable innovation. The very characteristics that have enabled our colleges to thrive for more than one hundred years—open access, low cost, convenience, community focus, and responsiveness to local demand—have also positioned them for strategic partnerships and early adoption of new technologies. The problem is that for opportunity and innovation to be pursued, people, organizations, and cultures must be ready for change—a state that currently seems to defy the best efforts of leaders.

Assuming that public investment in community colleges will be limited in the foreseeable future, building on the success of models that already exist may be a way to approach the future. Community colleges are remarkably adept at sensing and responding to market shifts, and they are opportunistic. Building on core strengths by reinvesting resources—both existing and new, such as public and private partnerships—in ways that lead to exponential returns will enable our colleges to expand capacity and improve their impact on learners and communities.

NOTES

1. Interview with Scott Bowman, Central Queensland University, Australia, January 2012.

2. Clayton M. Christensen, Michael B. Horn, Louis Caldera, and Louis Soares, "Disrupting College: How Disruptive Innovation Can Deliver Quality and Affordability to Postsecondary Education," Center of American Progress, April 2011, 2–3, 13.

3. Christensen, Horn, Caldera, and Soares, "Disrupting College," 14–18.

4. Robert Sheets, Stephen Crawford, and Louis Soares, "Rethinking Higher Education Business Models: Steps Toward a Disruptive Innovation Approach to Understanding and Improving Higher Education Outcomes," Center for American Progress, March 28, 2012, 3–5, http://www.americanprogress.org/issues/2012/03/higher_ed_business_models.html.   Sheets, Crawford, and Soares reference the analytical framework outlined by Christensen et. al.

5. Sheets, Crawford, and Soares, "Rethinking Higher Education Business Models," 3–6.

6. Sheets, Crawford, and Soares, "Rethinking Higher Education Business Models," 6.

7. Christensen, Horn, Caldera, and Soares, "Disrupting College, 3.

8. Christensen, Horn, Caldera, and Soares, "Disrupting College, 3.

9. Sheets, Crawford, and Soares, "Rethinking Higher Education Business Models," 6–7.

10. Sheets, Crawford, and Soares, "Rethinking Higher Education Business Models," 7.

11. James Rosenbaum, Julie Redline, and Jennifer Stephan, "Community College: The Unfinished Revolution," *Issues in Science and Technology* (Summer 2007), http://www.issues.org/23.4/rosenbaum.html (accessed June 7, 2012).

12. Rosenbaum, Redline, and Stephan, "Community College: The Unfinished Revolution," 51.

13. Rosenbaum, Redline, and Stephan, "Community College: The Unfinished Revolution," 51–53.

14. Rosenbaum, Redline, and Stephan, "Community College: The Unfinished Revolution," 51–53.

15. Rosenbaum, Redline, and Stephan, "Community College: The Unfinished Revolution," 51–52.

16. Rosenbaum, Redline, and Stephan, "Community College: The Unfinished Revolution," 52–53.

17. Rosenbaum, Redline, and Stephan, "Community College: The Unfinished Revolution," 52.

18. Rosenbaum, Redline, and Stephan, "Community College: The Unfinished Revolution," 52.

19. Daniel Pianko and Josh Jarrett, "Early Days of a Growing Trend: Nonprofit/For-Profit Academic Partnerships in Higher Education," in *Game Changers: Education and Information Technologies*, ed. Diana G. Oblinger (Lawrence: Allen Press, 2012), 98.

20. Pianko and Jarrett, "Early Days of a Growing Trend," 98.

21. Pianko and Jarrett, "Early Days of a Growing Trend," 99.

22. Interview with Scott Bowman, Central Queensland University, Australia.

23. USQ news release, July 28, 2011.

24. Interview with USQ vice chancellor Bill Lovegrove.

25. Nancy Zimpher, SUNY News Release, August 2011.

26. Lorain County Community College University Partnerships, http://www.lorainccc.edu/UP/Bachelor+and+Master+Degree+Programs/.

27. Davis Jenkins, "Redesigning Community Colleges for Completion: Lessons from Research on High-Performance Organizations," *CCRC Research Brief* 48, Community College Research Center, January 2011, 1.

28. Jenkins, "Redesigning Community Colleges for Completion," 2. Jenkins cites research on private-sector firms by Carr & Pearson, 1999; Kaynak, 2003; and Sezhiyan & Nambirajan, 2010.

29. Anthony P. Carnevale, Nicole Smith, and Jeff Strohl, *Help Wanted: Projections of Jobs and Education Requirements through 2018* (Washington, DC: Georgetown University Center on Education and the Workforce, 2010), 1, http://cew.georgetown.edu/JOBS2018/.

30. Carnevale, Smith, and Strohl, *Help Wanted*, 2010, 16.

31. Anthony P. Carnevale, Jeff Strohl, Michelle Melton, *What's It Worth? The Economic Value of College Majors* (Washington, DC: Georgetown University Center on Education and the Workforce, May 24, 2011), http://cew.georgetown.edu/whatsitworth/.

32. Business Roundtable, *Getting Ahead–Staying Ahead: Helping America's Workforce Succeed in the 21st Century*, The Springboard Project, 2009, 14–15, http://businessround-table.org/studies-and-reports/the-springboard-project-releases-final-recommendations-to-strengthen-a/.

33. Business Roundtable, *Getting Ahead–Staying Ahead*, 32.

34. Business Roundtable, *Getting Ahead–Staying Ahead*, 32.

35. John H. Pryor, Linda DeAngelo, Laura Palucki Blake, Sylvia Hurtado, and Serge Tran, "The American Freshman: National Norms Fall 2011," Higher Education Research Institute, University of California, Los Angeles, 2011, 9.

36. Carol Geary Schneider, "'Degrees for What Jobs?' Wrong Question, Wrong Answers," *The Chronicle of Higher Education*, May 1, 2011, http://chronicle.com/article/Degrees-for-What-Jobs-Wrong/127328/ (accessed May 25, 2011).

37. Business Roundtable, *Getting Ahead–Staying Ahead*, 18, based on a personal interview with Trina Condo, director of Florida Education and Training Placement Information Program, August 31, 2009.

38. Bloomberg.com/View, April 29, 2012.

39. Diana G. Oblinger, "IT as a Game Changer," in *Game Changers: Education and Information Technologies*, ed. Diana G. Oblinger (Lawrence: Allen Press, 2012), 37–51.

40. Oblinger, *Game Changers*, 40–41.

41. Oblinger, *Game Changers*, 41.

42. Paul E. Lingenfelter, "The Knowledge Economy: Challenges and Opportunities for American Higher Education," in *Game Changers: Education and Information Technologies*, ed. Diana G. Oblinger (Lawrence: Allen Press, 2012), 19.

Index